Search for Acceptance

The Adolescent and Self-Esteem

Search for Acceptance
The Adolescent and Self-Esteem

Janet Kizziar & Judy Hagedorn

Nelson-Hall/Chicago

nh

LIBRARY OF CONGRESS CATALOGING IN PUBLICATION DATA

Kizziar, Janet W.
    Search for Acceptance
    Bibliography: p.
    Includes index.
    1. Adolescent Psychology.   2. Social
Acceptance.   3. Self-Respect.   I.   Hagedorn,
Judy W., joint author.   II. Title.
BF724.K565   155.5   78-11491
ISBN 0-88229-369-9

Manufactured in the United States of America

10   9   8   7   6   5   4   3   2   1

To our grandfather, Vance H. Dunn, and to the memory of our grandmother, Gracia L. Dunn, who provided us with unconditional love.

To George D. Small, whose commitment to authenticity and personal involvement made learning a joy.

To the memory of Haim G. Ginott, who demonstrated humane precepts and perceptivity.

Contents

Preface

This book is, in part, a collection of our experiences and what we have learned from dealing intimately with adolescents and their families as psychologists and, more importantly, as friends. In these relationships we have found certain ideals essential: unqualified acceptance, emotional honesty, belief in others, and trust.

Although we do not intend to dispense advice, we do suggest alternatives for parents who want their children to feel more secure in following their personal choices and not those of the crowd. We feel that parents, educators, teenagers, and, for that matter, all who are interested in human personality and growth should find this book helpful. In addition, those who may be concerned that people are becoming increasingly less responsible for decisions affecting their lives should find the questions this book poses challenging.

Certainly our close relationship with the late Dr. Haim Ginott intensified our feelings that children must be treated with respect in order to develop respect for themselves, a condition essential to healthy self-esteem. Another great teacher, Dr. George D. Small, taught us never to underestimate any human's potential for growth, and we have yet to be disappointed.

We express our gratitude to our clients and friends who have shared with us their experiences, some of which helped to illustrate many of our premises.

We also wish to acknowledge our appreciation to Karen

Casillas and Richard Warzynski for the research they contributed to this work, and special thanks to our editors, Dorothy J. Anderson and Elizabeth Hansen.

In this book, rather than the rapidly becoming overworked device of "he/she" or continual use of the word "person," we'll use the pronoun "he." However, when specifically referring to a woman, we will use "she." (Our apologies to our sisters if this appears sexist, as it is not intended to be so.)

Prologue

We feel that an adolescent's self-evaluation is the single most important factor in determining his response to peer group pressure.

Adolescents with inadequate self-esteem most usually are those who follow the crowd and its dictates, disregarding the values and ideals instilled by their families. Their search, then, is for acceptance and security.

Certainly a warm and loving home environment helps many to resist negative peer influences, as may religious training and other factors. Research, however, indicates increasing numbers of young people are easily swayed by pressure and manipulation, and many are poorly equipped to go against the crowd.

The solution to this monumental problem is simple: We must create environments conducive to producing young people with healthy self-esteems.

> Living without pressure—without putting it on myself or others—without allowing others to put it on me. Living without strings, or selling, or charming, or kidding into compliance, or manipulating through niceness or threatened anger. Standing in the face of silence, and threats, and expectations, and misunderstandings —standing and gently saying "No thank you, I'll be myself."*
>
> —Hugh Prather

*From *I Touch the Earth, the Earth Touches Me.* Copyright © 1972 by Hugh Prather. Reprinted by permission of Doubleday & Company, Inc.

1 The Peer Group

Less than a year ago Leslie, age fifteen, was a delight to her parents. She was pleasant, thoughtful, responsible, and seemingly involved with family, friends, and school.

Without warning, she seemed transformed into a slovenly, moody recluse who is hostile and antagonistic toward her parents when she chooses to acknowledge them at all.

Labeling her parents "hopelessly outdated," she belittles their moral, political, and religious beliefs. She threatens to quit school, run away, live with her boyfriend, and hints that she may be experimenting with drugs. She seems to be intentionally attempting to aggravate her parents and they are becoming increasingly intolerant and bewildered. Leslie turns to her friends for companionship, solace, direction and love, while openly rejecting her family.

Leslie's concerned parents need to realize that she is probably working her way through the fairly normal conflicts of adolescence. Their strength, guidance, and humane treatment may greatly influence her self-understanding and help her to emerge a joyful, compassionate person with regard for others' feelings. Positive parental judgments and unqualified support are the most decisive factors in enabling young people to resist negative peer pressures. We need to learn to deal with and eventually prevent the unbearable tensions that so frequently exist between parents and their adolescents.

The way his peers perceive him strongly influences the adolescent's conception of himself, which generally remains unchanged throughout his life. Peer influences are at their zenith during preadolescence and adolescence when youngsters are most inclined to feel socially, emotionally, and even intellectually inept. During this interval they tend to seek endorsement and support from others. This period of transition from the dependence of childhood to the emotional, physical, and social maturity of young adulthood is typically estimated between the ages of twelve and twenty-one. Puberty, which is frequently one to three years earlier in girls than in boys, usually marks the outset of adolescence.

An adolescent is extremely vulnerable to judgments expressed by those in his immediate environment because he is at a period in his life where others' opinions are of tremendous importance in formulating his self-concept. A primary need of adolescents is acceptance by those significant in their environments—love in the home, esteem and regard among contemporaries and respect from teachers and employers. Young people seem to be basically social and most vehemently seek to become members of established groups, regardless of the price they may have to pay.

Comfort is vitally important in all primary relationships; when an adolescent feels accepted, he is spontaneous rather than apprehensive and he usually does not feel it necessary to prove himself. When they can be open, adolescents will probably mature from their experiences, but they also face the risk of rejection and subsequent lack of confidence in themselves. Individuals who have been hurt in their peer interactions usually tend to withdraw or to build up psychological defenses and protective barriers.

The discerning young person realizes that not everyone is to be solicited or even desired as a friend. Most adolescent attachments vary in stability and intensity, and a relatively secure teenager realizes that some of his peers will undoubtedly find him socially unacceptable at various periods of his life. Young people need to learn to accept these realities and to be unperturbed by fluctuations of status and prestige that accompany what is often referred to as "growing up."

The adolescent peer group, besides being a retreat from the world of adults, is also a setting where young people form strong attachments and where solidarity is protected by considerable conformity. The peer group further is the focus of a young person's life; what transpires there is generally most significant. Within peer groups, amity and allegiance are of prevailing importance, especially in the face of adult censure or contempt.

Young people tend to form their own particular cultures partially because they feel in a state of limbo—sometimes considered children and saddled with restrictions, and at other times regarded as adults, with more responsibilities than they are emotionally equipped to assume. If the adolescent is provided numerous opportunities for participation in responsible activities that require mature decision making, his induction into adult society will be smoother.

There is considerable merit in the adolescent's endeavor to find signficance and value in his life. His search for meaning thwarts uninvolved and ill-considered affirmation of accepted standards and traditions and broadens his understanding and judgments. The inherent risk is the youngster's tendency then to be aware only of society's defects and decadence and his tendency to withdraw with his peers in order to form an ideal community. There does seem to be a movement, however, toward adolescent involvement and commitment to exposing and altering the hypocrisies of their elders.

Increasing numbers of young people as they reach adolescence reject their mothers and fathers, virtually dissolving their relationships with them. Whether they leave physically

or psychologically, they are usually searching for more fulfilling alliances.

Disillusionment with family life tends to mirror the breakdown of relationships with family members. Young people
spend increasingly less time with their parents and siblings
and more with their peers. When at home they are usually
pursuing such activities as watching television, listening to
music, doing homework, talking on the telephone or closing
themselves in their rooms, always shunning any unessential
interaction with their families.

It is beneficial if parents recognize and understand that
adolescents change drastically and continually attempt to expand their boundaries beyond the home. When parents seek to
frustrate their children's needs for new friendships and experiences, the adolescents generally feel stifled and hostile and
probably will react with childish behaviors. This conduct often
reinforces to the parents that their adolescents are emotionally
immature and poorly equipped for the responsibilities and
privileges they desire. The loosening of parental ties must be
gradual and adapted to each young person's needs.

For rearing children there are no best methods; all that
exist are alternatives. But this may be axiomatic: Only when
a young person feels good can he be good. In other words,
when parents expect little from their youngster, his behaviors
will most likely conform to their aspirations.

Groups exercise pressure through control of admission to
their restricted circle. They often confine their membership to
those who comply to their dictates and many seek insidious
domination of those within their influence. Although groups
vary in size, intimacy, and requirements for membership, all
members are influenced by subtle or explicit communication
of values from one to another. The young person secure in his
position with his friends and family is more likely to be im-
mune to harassment, manipulation, or enticement by peers.
He can then operate independently; not as a programmed
robot or "yes man," a posture many adolescents assume to earn
acceptance and prestige.

CASE HISTORY

Julio, whose family migrated from Mexico when he was twelve years old, has difficulty with school and interpersonal relationships. At fourteen years of age, he is the oldest youngster in seventh grade, having failed twice, and his prognosis for passing this year is poor. He has been termed a "slow learner" although his partial language barrier may be the reason his intellectual potential measures at the low extreme of the normal range. Julio's classmates torment him, calling him "Wetback" and he challenges and fights with them before and after school. Although he is rather small for his age, he appears unafraid of a skirmish, even when several are against him. He is often late to school, rarely does homework and is impudent and hostile to his teachers. His family has little time for him—both parents work long hours and the other children in the family are older and no longer live at home. Julio has not received parental, school or peer support, so he will likely grasp at anything that will make him feel less alienated and lonely.

An adolescent's rejection of his parents' values is frequently his attempt to become autonomous and unlike his parents, to whom he has always been subordinate. Parents should endeavor to provide their youngsters with the security and courage to shape and pursue their personal convictions as they work their way toward maturity. It is absurd to keep exasperations and rage in check, because so doing implies one is more willing to risk destroying himself than dissolving a relationship. When with their peers, adolescents can avoid the pressure of feeling that they continually disappoint meaningful adults in their lives. Some young people feel that no matter how hard they try, they only aggravate or embarrass their elders.

As a young person matures, his strong family connections

tend to fray and become less cohesive. The adolescents then typically seek endorsement from each other. Their loyalties and crises are more intense and their relationships are often more secure than are those of most adults. Although they love and communicate, they can also pressure, censure, and ostracize one another.

Certainly many teenagers become more greatly pressured by the persuasions of their peers since they are without a real kinship with meaningful adults. These adolescents are easily swayed by the conducts, demands and challenges of their colleagues. Young people are searching for alliances with others so they can feel increasingly capable and less lonely.

It is difficult for parents to permit their children to feel differently than they do about specific issues and considerations. Too often parents subconsciously convey to their children: "You must feel as we do if you want us to love you." Instead, young people need unconditional acceptance and support, although their feelings and values are usually destined to be independent and distinct from those of their parents. Each family member should be valued for his own uniqueness. It is too difficult for adolescents, seeking parental approval, to live a relationship on the principle of pretense.

Parents need to try to give their children guidance in choosing their particular peer groups, and this is a most difficult task. They might suggest that although the social aspect is an important consideration, groups that revolve around mutual interests and responsible activities are apt to be more enriching, stimulating, and maturing to their members.

A healthy attitude for a young person to develop is that since some people will like him and some will not, if he is authentic those who do like him will be responding to the real person, not to an image or a role he is playing. When Michelangelo was asked how he created the beautiful statue David, he replied, "I took a block of granite, and I chipped away everything that was not David." This illustrates the quest for authenticity, which involves freeing ourselves from things that are *not* us.

Teaching their children to be genuine and honest is a primary goal of most parents. When parents operate from behind a facade, pretending to be serene and loving when they feel enraged and annoyed, they are setting poor examples. According to Dr. Carl Rogers, "The more fully an individual is understood and accepted, the more he tends to drop the false fronts with which he has been meeting life, and the more he tends to move in a direction which is forward."[1]

A primary objective of parents should be removing the barriers between themselves and their youngsters so that all can feel more safety in intimate mutual communication. When legitimate feelings can be expressed and shared, there is usually a reduction in defensiveness on all parties' parts. This is probably why adolescents can often speak more freely with each other—they feel no need to maintain an illusion or false impression.

Adults often attempt to pattern young people in their own images to prepare them for the demands and impositions of the current culture. Parents need, instead, to provide a concerned detachment to allow their children autonomy and freedom while simultaneously producing a sense of self-acceptance and value. Adolescents belong to their friends—and they risk, learn, and ripen by their ventures and mistakes. Much that they value their parents find repugnant and intimidating, so the young find in each other shelter from the agony and rage that threatens their selfhood and independence.

Young people are often far more capable and competent than their parents realize. Sometimes the restrictions they place on their adolescents are merely to preserve parental peace of mind, and these controls are unfair. Fortunately, most youngsters are resilient and recover rather rapidly from their parents' mistakes. To attain self-respect and self-reliance, adolescents must be given opportunities to rely on their own judgments.

The adolescent usually demonstrates a heightened interest in the opposite sex, and his strong sexual urges may promote frustrations and even guilt feelings. Usually mood swings are

---

[1]Carl R. Rogers, *On Becoming a Person*, p. 27.

pronounced, and seemingly trivial events can set off violent reactions. An additional problem is adaptation to an altered body image. In childhood, growth changes are gradually more rapid and more intimately related to emotional well-being. The adolescent feels he is "wearing" a different and strange kind of body, and since his body image is closely tied to his self-concept, he must go through a period of reconciling the new to the old. This is a complex process involving accentuated interest in the body, self-exploration, comparisons with others, preoccupation with personal appearance, concern over physical skill and health, and frequently conflict between a desire to display the body and an urge to conceal attributes that cause embarrassment.[2]

Youngsters are often extremely sensitive about any physical deviations from the norm, from an underdeveloped chest to a crooked nose. Often their peers provoke and scorn them, which serves to intensify their embarrassment. A large percentage seem to feel different and therefore consider themselves unacceptable to their peers for a myriad of reasons including their weight, height, skin condition, poor physique, poor eyesight, and the need to wear glasses, and late maturation of secondary sexual characteristics. Many continue to contend with their legitimate or imaginary imperfections or flaws throughout adulthood. Parents can assist by subtly encouraging them to accept their appearances while helping them to effect changes when feasible.

Many adults are unaware of or choose to disregard the reality that successful relationships with their peers are of primary importance to most adolescents. These relationships form the setting for each young person's existence and strongly influence his emotional adjustment and happiness.

---

[2]Robert M. Goldenson, *The Encyclopedia of Human Behavior: Psychology, Psychiatry, and Mental Health.* Copyright © 1970 by Robert M. Goldenson.

2 Self-Concept & Its Relationship to Self-Esteem

Although adolescents often appear unconcerned, it is usually extremely important to them that their friends approve of their appearance—even if peer standards vary greatly from those of their parents. Many young people state that adults attach far too much import to appearances. They feel that a person should be judged by what he is inside—not by his dress or the length of his hair. Yet, paradoxically, they are the sternest critics of appearance, which in many cases determines whether a young person is in the "in crowd" or out. When adolescents evaluate those of the opposite sex, appearance is at the top of the list as an important criterion. Throughout preadolescence and adolescence most young people are overly self-conscious about the impressions they make on others, both members of the opposite sex and of the same sex. To be acceptable to his peer group, a young person must not differ too much from others in physical appearance. Overreaction on this issue by

"SORRY SALLY, SOMETHING ABOUT YOU JUST DOESN'T FIT IN WITH OUR GROUP. YOU'RE JUST NOT WITH IT."

Taffy Wright West

both parties is typical. A young person who is angry at his parents for dictating what he must wear and how he should look often rebels and does the opposite of what they demand. Parents who overemphasize the necessity for proper and respectable attire may find that their children will wear nothing but patched jeans and tee shirts. In addition they may bathe infrequently and wear their hair in the style most repugnant to their parents.

Parents frequently find that they are far more persuasive when they request rather than demand that their teenagers dress appropriately. Compromises in dress may ease the tension. There is really no legitimate reason why a young lady should not be allowed to dress casually at school if she conforms to the school dress code. A young man should not be forced to wear extremely short hair simply because his parents prefer it, when all of his friends wear a longer style. When adolescents know that within certain boundaries they are granted the right to make their own decisions about dress, they will probably cooperate when their parents request special attire or changes in their appearances.

It is easy for adults to forget how important peer acceptance is to adolescents and what an important part appearance plays in gaining admission to the group. When an adolescent differs significantly from his friends and classmates, they may never give him the opportunity to show that he might be a welcome addition to their crowd.

CASE HISTORY

Melinda, a high school sophomore, desperately sought acceptance from her peers. She was both physically and socially immature, and was forced to dress as if she were still in grade school. Her parents were reluctant to see their only child become a young woman, so they became overly protective and treated her as if she were much younger. Her classmates either ignored her or teased her cruelly, calling her a baby and even a queer. She reacted initially with tears and finally withdrew from any unnecessary interaction with her classmates. A perceptive school counselor called Melinda in for a conference and found her receptive and eager to discuss her problem. Since much of her conflict was related to her immature appearance, the counselor felt that a session with her parents might be productive. When Melinda's parents gained insight into her situation, they cooperated by helping her to dress more in the styles worn by her peers. Certainly changes in her clothing and hairstyle did not provide Melinda with instant self-confidence, maturity, or peer acceptance, but gradually, with the counselor's support, she made some friends and ceased to be the class scapegoat.

Not infrequently, adolescents have chosen to drop out of school or to run away rather than to obey a parental decree that would make them differ significantly in appearance from their peers.

One more ingenious fourteen-year-old boy, whose father nagged constantly about his hair, bragged, "Since I've had my ears pierced and wear these earrings, he's stopped mentioning the length of my hair. He probably lives in mortal fear of the day I'll cut my hair and expose my ear lobes." When asked if he wanted to wear earrings, he admitted he did not, "but it serves him [father] right! Whatever he can choose to get on my back about, I'll stay one step ahead of him!"

Many researchers have found that early maturing boys and girls appear to have higher self-esteems than do late bloomers. Early maturation is particularly important to males, and correlations are high between such personality components as dominance, aggression, responsibility, and early maturation.

All of us—children, adolescents, and adults—perceive ourselves in large measure from the feedback we get from others. If as a child one receives inputs from parents and significant others in the family setting that make him feel secure, attractive, loved, and capable—an "I count" person—he develops a positive self-concept. If, on the other hand, the inputs from his peer group, teachers, and neighbors are that he is a failure, or ugly or obese, he may tend, in spite of his ideal early environment, to grow up not liking himself much. As he matures, inputs continue to come from people important in the youngster's eyes and they confirm or alter his self-concept, instilling both negative and positive attitudes toward himself.

Even without training in psychological testing one can capture some of the feelings of self-worth or lack of same by studying these pictures drawn by three fourteen-year-old girls. The size of the drawings, placement on the pages, and movement of the body all have obvious connotations. The faint, hesitant lines speak for themselves as well. Often such drawings, along with other projective devices, help professionals to identify nonverbal clues pertaining to feelings of inadequacy, inferiority, depression, hostility, poor body image, and evasion, as well as more intangible personality variables.

A prime reason for many young people's lack of self-confidence is being overweight. Parents can either contribute to the
overweight adolescent's problem, or they can furnish subtle
assistance in helping him to lose. Of course, this problem could
possibly have been avoided had proper eating habits been instilled from early childhood. This certainly is not to imply a
guarantee against extra poundage in the preteen and teen
years however, since troubled children, particularly those who
are alienated by their peers, often find comfort in eating.

A parent who continually makes reference and calls attention to his teenager's weight problem will find that if a change in eating habits results, it is usually a change for the worse. It is far more beneficial to have a private discussion to determine how to best handle this problem.

If they feel that they must discuss this situation, parents usually hear from their adolescent a denial of concern about his weight or a refusal to acknowledge his weight problem. This

is seldom how the youngster really feels, however. More likely he is very sensitive and embarrassed and prefers to avoid even thinking about his weight. If the teenager agrees to tackle his weight problem, a visit to the family doctor for both a physical and a go-ahead on the diet plan is in order.

It is extremely detrimental to nag or to criticize if the teenager strays from his diet—as he will be apt to do. Ideally, he would come to his parents with his concerns about his weight, but since usually it is the other way around, he may be "going off the wagon" for retaliatory purposes. ("This wasn't my idea, so I'll show them!")

The reasons experts have given for overeating are numerous: to relieve tension, as a substitute for love, to make up for the loss of a loved one, to discourage sexual involvement because the obesity makes one less physically attractive to others, to avoid conflict by not threatening others with one's attractiveness, to compensate for some childhood deprivation —the list could go on and on. Whatever the underlying causation, it is usually more helpful to attack the result; and undoing the obesity and the excessive eating is not easy. Also there is no miracle cure, notwithstanding some of the ads one reads in magazines and newspapers.

Although much has been researched about obesity and its effect on self-esteem, little is written about the extremely thin individual—perhaps since they are outnumbered in our overweight society. However, an extremely skinny, shapeless adolescent often suffers from low self-esteem and is the object of as much ridicule as is the overweight adolescent. Here again, the weight problem can usually be overcome with the advice of the family doctor coupled with proper diet, exercise, and rest. Too often the underweight child thinks the solution is to eat as much "junk" food as possible (that it, soft drinks, french fries, and candy bars); but this seldom works and is usually self-defeating.

Many child development specialists feel that the child's perception of his own body becomes the nucleus of the awareness of the self. If a young person fits well into our cultural ideal of the slim, well-proportioned physique, he probably will have a healthy self-concept, but if he is self-conscious about his body, low self-esteem and feelings of inferiority are generated.

Acne usually is devastating to a young person's self-confidence and should be treated as quickly as possible. Reminding him to cut out chocolate and soft drinks until he outgrows the situation is not a viable solution. Many parents do not know how traumatizing their youngster's breakouts are to him: "How can he get so upset—even breaking a date, when

I can't see a thing wrong with his face! It's ridiculous!" To the adolescent boy, anxiety about his date probably added to his flare-up, and his parents' taking it so lightly was probably even more devastating.

Parents can help by assuring a proper diet, by treating his problem as confidentially as possible and by taking their adolescent to a dermatologist if the situation requires it. Certainly nagging does not help. Many new studies indicate that diet does not play as major a role in complexion problems as once thought. "I spent all my good money on the dermatologist, and here you aren't even following his advice!" How much better would be: "It's tough, if not impossible, to lay off the chocolate entirely. I sure couldn't 'cold turkey' it when I was dieting."

Young people with physical impairments are often teased or ostracized by their peers—or they may be simply treated differently, which they report is equally disturbing. Adolescents who are confined to wheelchairs, those who are partially sighted, those who must use hearing aids, or those with speech impediments frequently suffer when with their peers; and their parents typically are the last to know. These youngsters are past masters at "keeping a stiff upper lip" and denying that they are in pain, either physical or emotional. They often team with those they perceive as other outcasts and usually have extremely low self-concepts. If they are able to excel in some area or endeavor they often make gains in self-esteem and in peer acceptance.

The young person termed a "slow" learner, whether this is due to mental retardation, a learning disability, or an emotional difficulty often has the same psychological profile as does the child with a physical impairment. He quickly learns that he is *different*—a social misfit—except perhaps when with those sharing his own special problem. He has strong feelings of inadequacy. He frequently denies his unhappiness and feelings of alienation to his family. Until this young person can be made to feel worthy he will continue perceiving himself as unacceptable to his peers. When adequate gains in self-esteem are made, his negative feelings about himself may lessen somewhat.

Unfortunately the extremely bright youngster must often disguise his intelligence to gain peer acceptance. The "brain" is usually excluded and ridiculed, particularly in the junior high school years. In the past, many girls traditionally conceded by "playing dumb" for male acceptance, but in the light of the women's movement the majority seem to be discarding previously accepted games women played. The preadolescent male does not escape from ostracism either, when his scholastic performance tops the achievements of his peers. Boys as well as girls have complained that they are unable to perform as well as they might in the classroom setting, since by doing so they subject themselves to rejection and rebuke from their classmates. Few preadolescents are secure enough to risk exclusion by excelling scholastically and hence out-matching their peers.

For the young person going through an awkward stage, dancing lessons frequently aid in developing grace and assurance. The confidence youngsters gain in ballroom dancing classes promotes social facility and ease with the opposite sex. These lessons should not start too early or be forced on the child, however. Other alternatives helpful to some include modeling courses, exercise classes, and yoga. The benefits of acquiring good posture and graceful body movements often aid a shy, inept youngster in overcoming excessive self-consciousness. When he feels that he projects a more poised image, a young person often experiences increasing confidence within his peer group.

A teenager with little sense of self-worth and personal identity tends to be dependent and conforming and frequently reflects the personalities of those with whom he associates. Certainly those who are particularly susceptible to peer influence need encouragement to develop self-sufficiency, which correlates highly with both ego strength and healthy esteem. Young people who perceive themselves as estranged from their peers, or those who are not totally accepted due to poor body images or because they are unable to dress or to perform to their peers' exacting standards, find this self-sufficiency difficult, if not impossible, to attain. Since they crave acceptance so desperately, they typically remain "people pleasers," content to balance precariously on the fringe edge of the group, following its orders and dictates and going along with its customs, for to oppose them would be to risk ostracism.

A child's body image plays a much greater role in his relationships with his peers and his general adaptation to his environment than once was believed, and it is influenced tremendously by his family's attitude. If they are overly concerned, stress the growing-up process prematurely, worry when their child does not have friends, or compare him with their own ego ideal; parents may find their child doubting his developing sense of being a person with his own value.

3 The Importance of Early Childhood

Most child guidance experts will agree that for a youngster to enjoy an emotionally satisfying adulthood one of the best guarantees is to provide an emotionally satisfying early childhood.

Children switch from extrovertive to withdrawal stages between the ages of two and five. Parents should be aware of these behavioral swings and realize that they are normal stages of development. They should further realize that the shy, withdrawn preschooler should not be pushed into settings where he might be uncomfortable; nor should the outgoing show-off continually be stifled.

Parental attitudes are probably the most significant influence in the establishment of the preschooler's personality. When parents are overly protective or domineering their children are usually shy, anxious, or submissive. Children from secure and cooperative homes are typically emotionally strong, happy, and extrovertive in nature.

When one parent gives the child one message, and the other parent a conflicting one, the child becomes confused since he needs approval from both. Certainly this happens occasionally in almost every family, but when parents constantly disagree about all aspects of child rearing, the child is apt to become tense and quarrelsome himself.

Compromise between what one parent sees as too strict and the other as too lenient is frequently the only solution for the child's benefit. When the parents present a united front the child will not fear the loss of love from either, and this is far preferable to the constant friction and conflict engendered when parents cannot declare a truce.

Children treated with fairness by their parents normally grow to respect the rights of others. Those receiving conflicting signals and who are not helped to deal with their feelings of resentment and confusion may either grow overtly hostile or withdrawn.

When a child learns during his earliest years that he can depend on his parents when he really needs them, he will feel secure. With the advantages of this ideal early environment, he will more readily reach out to others in similar trust and with positive expectations.

Many parents expect too much of their young children, not waiting until they are ready to pursue activities such as walking, riding a tricycle, or playing baseball. They instead tend to push them into such experiences, usually to satisfy their own ego needs—to be able to say such things as "Certainly, Sherrill has known her alphabet since she was two and one-half. Doesn't Tommy know his yet?"

Such pressure, coupled with unrealistic expectations of either or both parents, may result in the child's thinking that he can never quite achieve or excel to the degree that he should, that he is unworthy. His self-esteem will certainly suffer and this is not an area that can easily be elevated by praise, reinforcement, or even years of psychological treatment.

Parents who do not realize that possessiveness is a normal aspect of development, as are exaggeration, stubbornness, negativeness, and countless other undesirable qualities, often feel their children will grow into selfish, willful, or compulsive individuals. They try to force sharing and punish their children for fantasizing or refusing to comply with their requests. Stressing the concept of sharing as soon as the child is old enough to comprehend is extremely helpful. This is more easily taught in a peer setting than with other siblings in the family. Insisting that a young child refrain from behaving in what a parent perceives as a socially unacceptable manner and constantly punishing him for the same may bring about even more undesirable symptoms.

Those children who are "too good," self-effacing, and in-gratiating are often fearful of their aggressive emotions and of their parents' retaliation. They transform these feelings into their opposites, never allowing their impulses to gain expression. These young people become totally involved with placating their parents, so they are unable to establish peer relationships or to assert themselves. They must be helped to express their negative feelings and to find their true identities, sometimes necessitating professional assistance. Often these are the children who are overlooked, since they appear so loving, compliant, and obedient.

How parents handle discipline deeply affects the young child's self-concept. If he feels unloved and resentful, he may tend to deceive himself and others about his true feelings by shifting the blame, taking out his hostility on smaller children or finding fault with others. Since ridiculing and humiliating a young child often make him feel impotent, enraged, and alienated, most child guidance experts find these techniques particularly harmful. A youngster can be disciplined with his self-respect intact by inviting his compliance and by explaining that it is the child's behavior that is disliked—not the child himself. When discipline of a very young child is extremely harsh or painful, he tends to forget what he is being disciplined for and to remember only that he wants revenge. This feeling may persist into adolescence and even adulthood, although the individual affected is usually totally unaware of its origin. Many young children who are overly restricted become discipline problems as do adolescents who are too closely supervised.

At every age level, but most particularly at preschool age, children experience a conflict between the wish to be adult and the wish to remain children. Regressive behavior is frequently seen in children when a new baby is added to the family, when they must start school, or when they are frustrated or tired. This backsliding happens to almost all young children and should be regarded by parents as a normal part of growth. When they treat regression as something wrong, meriting punishment, parents engender guilt in their children. Most children will soon regain their momentum if their childish behaviors are accepted and understood by their parents.

Around the age of four most children are fascinated with death. Some parents feel that this denotes deep depressive suicidal urges or morbidity, and become unduly concerned about where they went wrong. The same holds true when the youngster has nightmares, a fear of the dark, masturbates excessively, is afraid of people—this list could go on and on. Often the preschooler picks up on his parents' anxiety about his so-called problem and this may even serve to reinforce his behavior. A calm, matter-of-fact acceptance of the child's fear, anxiety, or activity his parents see as threatening is certainly the desirable response.

Since an interest in eating precedes an interest in people, and because infants learn to associate people with the relief of their hunger pangs, their initial and frequently permanent perception of social interaction develops during mealtime. Either others are accepting and nurturant, or they are perceived as authoritarian, anxious, and even rejecting. Some scientists feel that the early feeding situation is the matrix from which all forms of social, verbal, and adaptive behavior are derived.

Studies of normal eating patterns and emotional needs of young people suggest that parents should refrain from becoming excessively concerned at mealtime and that their primary responsibilities are to establish a relaxed mealtime atmosphere and then, quite simply, to let the children alone.

At preschool ages, most youngsters are egocentric. Because of their intellectual limitations, they are unable to put themselves in other children's positions. For example, they cannot understand when their mothers or fathers are sick and unable to play with them—they just keep begging and demanding that they play. Many parents would label their youngsters thoughtless and insensitive rather than intellectually immature. However, these children are incapable of putting themselves in their parents' positions and comprehending their need for quiet and rest.

Many preteens and teenagers vividly recall their parents' reactions to some of their early childhood behaviors, and remember being made to feel ashamed or inadequate for these very normal aspects of development.

CASE HISTORY

David, age seventeen, is a loner, and not by choice. He has few friends; none of the opposite sex. He admitted that he thought of the sex act as ugly: "Something animals do. It makes me ill to think about it." After months of counseling he recalled an incident with his little sister where he "played doctor" when he was approximately six, and his mother's reaction. The source of his attitudes toward sex was revealed as were his own feelings of guilt and self-loathing. "I remember her calling me an animal—telling me how despicable and dirty I was. She made me promise not to touch a girl. I guess all this time I've been hating the thought of sex, females in general and particularly myself."

Love and affection are best demonstrated to a preschool child physically. Undemonstrative parents, uncomfortable showing their feelings by kisses and hugging, may do their children a great disservice by avoiding such behavior. All the words of love a child can comprehend at his young age seldom compensate for this lack. Children growing up without receiving an overt display of affection from their parents often find it difficult in later years to give or express affection themselves. They frequently tend to feel unloved and subsequently unlovable, and perceive themselves as unacceptable to their peers in adolescence and adulthood.

To the preschool child, adults appear to be giants—giants who can roar with anger and mete out punishment. The young child perceives the world as oversized and himself as insignificantly small. The preschooler also typically sees adults as either good or bad, as they are in fairy tales.

In their earliest years children can be guided by their parents toward social sensitivity, leadership, and expressing their emotions in desirable manners. Their feelings toward authority figures are typically established in their formative years. Some may determine that authority is to be blindly obeyed while others may flaunt it. Parents and surrogate parents (preschool teachers, Sunday school teachers, grandparents) should steer children to both self-sufficiency and appropriate, realistic attitudes toward authority. Social interaction, at least in the early years of life, has a pronounced effect on a person's self-perception. Whereas children enter school with feelings about themselves almost totally based on parental evaluations, these feelings can be changed for the better. Studies show that children from stable homes with parents who are loving and supportive are seldom hurt by a poor scholastic environment, and those from emotionally impoverished homes usually profit from their associations with peers and teachers from more stable backgrounds.

The parents of preschoolers who do not afford their children opportunities to relate to others of their age group cannot expect that when they enter school their children will have instant excellent peer acceptance and approval. Those who have played with others, apart from their own siblings, have already learned much about the give-and-take and sharing involved in meaningful interaction with those of their own age. Youngsters not afforded these experiences tend to be shy in group settings with their peers, or overly aggressive and belligerent. Neither of these extremes ingratiates them with their group and they are often cruelly ostracized. Frequently they do not forget this early rejection and decide either that they do not need others or that they are socially unacceptable. These decisions may never be altered in later life.

A parent should observe whether his child is relating to his peers typically in an assertive or passive role and help him to modify his behavior at times. Being a leader is perceived by most parents as desirable unless the child maintains this posture by bullying and threatening other youngsters. A passive child must be taught more autonomy; he must be guided toward independence by telling him that he need not blindly obey the leader or by moving him into a new setting. Some parents, however, steer their children from group to group, finding each unacceptable in some way. The others may be too rough for their child, or too immature. For example one parent withdrew her two-and-one-half-year-old daughter from an excellent preschool which she described as "not intellectually challenging" for her. When parents constantly find their children's playmates unacceptable, particularly when they are enjoying their play, these children tend to feel different and apart from others. Certainly parents must be selective when arranging activities for their preschooler, but when they perceive their child as the epitome of all the virtues and other youngsters as not quite measuring up, they only help to have their child ostracized by his peers. In addition, a child who is constantly told that he is superior to others may find it difficult to measure up to his parents' expectations and may even shun his peers in an effort to prove to his parents that he is bored by their childish behavior. He may develop strong feelings of inadequacy or set himself apart, assuming the role of a loner in order to please his parents.

Preschool boys who are not allowed to mix with girls of this age and girls who aren't allowed to be with boys often are uncomfortable in boy-girl situations in later years. Parents who reinforce: "You wouldn't want to play ball with *girls*, would you? The other guys will think that you're a sissy!" are making a big mistake. The boy-girl roles should definitely be downplayed, if not forgotten, and the person-to-person roles stressed. Many excessively shy preteens and teens reveal that they were discouraged from being with those of the opposite sex in their early years.

Parents who push their young children into following in their footsteps often find that they achieve the opposite of the desired results. The artist who forces his child to draw, the professional athlete who decides his son will be an Olympic star, the perfect homemaker who wants her daughter to learn early the "housewifely arts"—all find that the more they belabor the point, the more turned off the child becomes.

Parents who had goals they did not achieve because they were not afforded opportunities by their parents often try to live vicariously through their children by urging them in these directions. These parents usually find that their children will not be molded into carbon copies of them nor will they become what their parents wanted to be when they grew up. They typically will lean in opposite directions, resisting parental urgings and persuasions and resenting attempts to mold them into what they are not. If they do comply, these children usually become progressively passive and compliant as they mature. These are the young people who readily succumb to peer pressures since they have learned since childhood that the way to please is through compliance.

The Harvard Preschool Project is a study of young children from birth to six years of age attempting to determine why some parents are more successful than others. Although the project is incomplete, in the ten years since its inception it has pointed to many useful suggestions for parents who want to help their children get the most from their preschool years. The Harvard Project's personnel suggest parents use words as often as possible, selecting vocabulary that may be a little too hard as well as words the child understands. In addition, a parent should be nearby and available to react to the child's activities at least half of his waking hours. Parents must teach their child that the world does not revolve around him; that they cannot always stop what they are doing to fulfill his requests. They are advised not to give in to unreasonable demands or to let temper tantrums intimidate them. Parents are cautioned to be firm and consistent in discipline and, perhaps in our opinions the most useful advice: Remember that you, the parents, are in charge and do not worry that your children will withhold their love if you have to refuse something.

Although it may be frustrating for parents to allow their child to do things for himself after they have fed, entertained, and clothed him for years, they should try to appreciate his feelings. He is discovering "I am me" and an early way to learn this successfully is by doing things for himself. Although it takes longer to wait for him to tie his own shoes, this reflects his newfound sense of self and initiative. This also develops new motor skills, and if parents in their impatience always step in to help, a child feels unable to take care of himself and this prolongs dependency.

Dependency in children's early years is often transferred to the peer group by the time they reach adolescence. These youngsters, because of their upbringing, believe themselves incapable of making independent decisions, so they look to their contemporaries for guidance and direction. They are followers because they were taught, albeit unwittingly, that they were incapable of using their own common sense and judgment.

A young child really does want to get along with his peers. If he receives their attention and they accept what he has to offer he has no need to overact, belittle, show off or boss other children to prove himself. A child who feels likable gives of himself more readily and accepts limits with less resentment. Parents should continually reinforce their child's self-esteem to help him like both himself and others better.

When a preschooler is continually confronted with his faults and shortcomings or with overly demonstrative affection and coddling, emotional strain occurs. Defects in the emotional maturity of his parents create most of the difficulties in the child's emotional growth.

When parents create conditions conducive to self-realization, their children will grow to find joy in being considerate to others.

Parents who demonstrate their trust and love to their children, accepting their conflicting emotions, help them to grow in emotional security and self-esteem. In spite of parents' best efforts, however, some problems are unavoidable. No doubt, parental attitudes greatly influence the ultimate resolution of these conflicts and their concomitant effects on children.

4 Family Intervention Through Family Interaction

Probably the biggest complaint from adolescents is: "I can't talk with my parents." Certainly the most frequently heard comment from parents is: "I can't communicate with my adolescent." Teenagers frequently believe that their parents are only capable of criticism, censure, and blame; while the parents often feel their children mock and condemn their values and standards. Is it possible, then, for the two generations to share a relevant dialogue? Probably,—if each will learn to listen, withholding value judgments until the other party has had the opportunity to fully express his feelings.

Parents are less likely than are adolescents to reveal family grievances and conflicts since their generation tends to feel these problems should remain in the privacy of the home. Perhaps they are less vocal about their children's shortcomings because this might suggest that they were not all that successful as parents. Adolescents, on the contrary, rarely feel at fault for a breakdown in parent-child relations—after all, "they didn't ask to be born."

CASE HISTORY

"When I try to explain the changing sexual mores, my mother begins name-calling. Even when I attempt to tell her that I am not practicing this new morality, she is unwilling to hear me out. If she never exposes herself to any new ideas or philosophies, how can she gain in understanding? I'm just trying to get through to her."

The mother of this teenaged girl indicated that her adolescent loved to get the whole family into a turmoil by making outlandish statements during what could be a peaceful dinner hour. "She'll say, 'Sex before marriage is preferable to what your generation did because we're smart enough to know we'd better sample the goods before we buy them.' This drives my husband up the wall, which is, of course, her objective. He becomes irate, yells at her, and I then attempt to make peace. When I say, 'She doesn't really mean that,' she retorts hostilely, 'Yes, I do.' She is then asked by her father or me to leave the table, which she does with a rather superior, condescending look. I can't conceive that there will ever be a day when we can have a mother-daughter talk about anything more profound than her hanging up her clothes. She has no respect for her parents, and we don't know how we can do anything about it. I never envisioned this happening in my family."

Her daughter's comment was that when she opened her mouth she could only expect moralizing and punishment from her parents, so the logical thing to do was to stop trying to explain her feelings to anyone except her peers.

Typically parents are hurt when their adolescents quit confiding in them, yet, on the adolescent's part, this phenomenon is understandable. They do not want moralizing; nor do they seek blame. What they are most frequently looking for is a listener—preferably one who is nonjudgmental. They want to try out their new philosophies and ideas on other human beings whose values they respect. If their parents close their ears, the young people will certainly try communicating with someone else, unfortunately usually one with no more experience or judgment than they themselves possess.

If the breakdown in communication between adolescent and parent is severe and if the young person seems to be experiencing problems with which he needs some counsel from others than his peers, professional guidance may be beneficial. Certainly a member of the clergy, a teacher, or even a relative or close family friend can attempt to talk with the adolescent, and often relationships of this nature are invaluable. In more complex situations, psychological or psychiatric counsel should be sought. No young person should be without a concerned adult he can talk with freely, and if he has no one, it is up to the parents to find such an individual.

Many young people are too threatened by rejection to disagree with their peers about anything. Several have admitted condoning acts of their friends, because to deny agreement would set them apart or even bring about ostracism:

Bill, age thirteen, said, "I agreed that running away was the only solution, since everybody else thought so. If I'd said, 'What if you get caught?' or, 'Why not try to last it out until you're eighteen?', the others would have thought I was some kind of Establishment freak. I couldn't risk it." Sally, age sixteen, said, "I kept up this big front about how cool it was for my boyfriend and his gang to rip off car parts, even though it was scaring me to death! When he spent his money from all that on me, I felt even guiltier. But I had to keep telling him how sharp they were and how much courage they all had, or he would have left me." Marcia, age fifteen, said, "I've got to pretend that I'm not a virgin and that sex is great if the two people are open and honest with each other. My group doesn't even think they have to be in love, or particularly even care that much about their sexual partner. Sex is just another way of relating to a fellow being. It goes against all of my feelings, but they'd ditch me if they thought I wasn't with it. I've gotten by so far by faking illness or pretending an out-of-town boyfriend was here. I just hope they never find out the truth because I sure talk a good game."

Peers tend to support, to agree, and to be the proverbial yes-men to their members' thoughts and ideas. Even as adults it is far more ego-satisfying to converse with another who concurs, encourages, compliments, and even applauds our words than one who ridicules and rejects them—or goes so far as to say that we have no idea what we are talking about. Someone who puts down our ideas will seldom be given the opportunity to hear them a second time. In fact, many will go out of their way to avoid any association with one who disagrees with his viewpoint. Yet parents wonder why their teenagers are never home, or when home, they are behind closed doors in their rooms, isolating themselves from the rest of the family.

If a youngster is contemplating using drugs, for example, to "expand his awareness," his peers are likely to agree that this is the answer. If he even intimated to his parents that he was considering drug experimentation, most probably they would ground him, forbid him to see his friends, and impose other restrictions. It is little wonder, then, that adolescents do not try out more of their new ideas on their parents. If this same adolescent had parents who would hear him out, they might, after listening to him, suggest other alternatives for him to consider. If these parents could listen to his feelings and explore with him why he felt this need to expand his awareness, perhaps together they could arrive at an answer acceptable to both.

Rosenbaum feels that a youngster should be allowed to express his feelings, but that parents should not be surprised if he does an about face the next day. She continues that a young person should not be rebuked if he does change his mind since adolescence is a time of experimentation. She advises parents "not to take apparent attacks personally. They are merely the youngster's way of saying, 'I'm different! Can you accept me as I am without making me feel foolish and insignificant?' "[1]

Many young people express a real need to "get through" to their parents. Although some have a desire to feel misunderstood, inexplicable, and remote, the vast majority want their mothers and fathers to understand their attitudes and standards of conduct. Their only problem seems to be how to communicate these feelings without the inevitability of a verbal

---

[1]Veryl Rosenbaum, "Guidelines for Parents Hoping to Survive Their Child's Adolescence," pp. 25–27. *PTA Magazine,* Nov. 1974.

attack from their parents: "I try to let them know that although we have tried their generation's standards and values, we found them false, at least for us. I verbalize this in as noncondemning a way as possible. I am immediately hit with the 'Where did we go wrong?' bit and I leave the room ashamed of how I've hurt my parents. Yet I know what's right for me was not right for them. I hate to pretend that I've embraced their morality and ideals. That's not fair either, but what can I do? I can either lie or state my position. Either way I feel guilty. I can't win."

Teenagers frequently complain that their parents pretend to listen and hear only what they want to hear: "She wants to think that I'm happy, popular, and carefree so she tells all of her friends that this is the case. When I try to tell her of my loneliness and desperation, she tells me that this too will pass and then ends with a charming anecdote of her changing from a moth to a butterfly at the age of sixteen. She's full of platitudes, but gives no support or consolation. No involvement. She doesn't take me seriously. Any moment I expect she'll tell me the Cinderella story—that we'll live happily ever after. I think she's afraid to stop talking—afraid that something I say will soak in and she'll discover the misery I'm in. So she chatters—aimlessly, meaninglessly—I've finally succeeded in shutting her out. When your own mother can't understand you, you really feel alienated."

One mother said, "I ask my daughter if she'd like to have a little talk, and she queries, 'What about?' I reply, 'Oh, anything,' and then she says, 'Why? What could the two of us possibly have to discuss?' "

Although the superior, condescending air many adolescents affect hurts parents deeply, they should realize it is often a cover-up, a facade. Youngsters who have been made to feel guilty for their ideas will likely avoid any confrontation or conversation more controversial than the weather forecast.

So many complain that all they hear is that they have it made—that if they had had to live in their parents' generation they'd have known: what it was to be hungry; the meaning of a dollar; respect; to listen to what their parents had to say;

and to keep their mouths shut until they knew what they were talking about. One parent remarked, "My friends' youngsters really think I am great. For some reason they can open up to me and tell me their innermost thoughts and feelings without fearing my criticism or worrying that I'll tell their parents. Why can't I be this way with my own children? When they express a viewpoint other than one I embrace, I jump down their throats. I become defensive immediately and our conversation ends in tears or with someone walking out. I don't want to rear my youngsters as carbon copies of myself, but somehow I am unable to tolerate any deviation from my standards in my own children. I know that this is breeding hostility between us, but I am at a loss."

All parents must accept the reality that their children will not become absolute reproductions of themselves in thoughts, feelings, moralities, and actions. If they can regard these differences in their children as normal assertions of independence, they will be less apt to feel that they have failed as parents.

That many adolescents may look up to their parents as models rather than rejecting them may be inferred from Joseph Woefel's research. This five-year study of high school students revealed that when asked to list the names of individuals who were important to them, first choice for boys usually was their fathers; girls, their mothers. The opposite sexed parent usually rated in third place. Woefel said "expectations, not hopes, of significant others was the single most important factor which influenced teenagers" in their attitudes, expectations, achievements, and job choices.[2]

CASE HISTORY

Roger, age fifteen: "Every time I complain about anything, I hear how I've got it made. If I have one hour of homework, I have to listen to my dad tell about four

---

[2]Joseph Woefel, "Adolescent-Adult Bond," p. 468. *School and Society,* Dec. 1971.

to six hours of assignments he completed every evening in high school. If I ask for the car, he'll tell about riding a bicycle until he graduated from college. If I even decline a serving of vegetables, I'll hear how lucky I am that there is more on the table than soup, which he apparently had for dinner every evening. It has evolved into a game of sorts. I guess at times I bait him, but I'm so tired of being hit on the head about how grateful I should be for all of the advantages afforded me. I guess he wants me to kiss his feet and tell him what a wonderful guy he is. I can't. I just resent him more and more. I play the Spoiled Brat to his Martyred Father. This show plays daily, and we are never off stage."

CASE HISTORY

Charlotte, age eighteen: "I simply quit talking to my mother. So many conversations ended with her crying and my feeling terrible. She made me feel guilty continually. Since the divorce she's made no effort to meet people or to go out at all. I became her sole companion and each time I left I'd have to think of her sitting alone all evening, ready to lay on the guilt as I walked in the door: 'I thought someone was trying to break into the house earlier, but, of course, my only child was out. God knows where. I could have been killed!' This was a typical introduction to most of our conversations since the divorce. I then became defensive: 'I have the right!' She would martyr herself more, dissolve into tears and I would rush out of the room. We'd begin again the next day. Now I won't be drawn into these scenes. I ignore her references to my heartlessness and lack of feeling for her. I don't let myself show anger or resentment. I calmly make some meaningless statement such as, 'Looks like rain.' I'm sorry, but it's all that works."

Many teenagers state that although they can easily come
to their parents with their victories and triumphs, they cannot contemplate discussing a defeat or humiliation. Some
typical comments are: "I guess I couldn't stand their pity."
"I don't want it oversimplified and I certainly couldn't bear
a 'You're young—you'll get over it in another six months.'
They mean well, but they'd overcompensate. Dad would slip
me five bucks and mother would bake a cake, but no one
would mention my agony."

When asked what they did want, since their dissatisfac-
tions covered a wide range of responses, most indicated that
all they needed was a sympathetic listener. They emphasized
that they wanted the topic dropped after the discussion, not
thrown back at them later: "Remember six weeks ago when
you said you'd never love again?" "Do you recall being so depressed when you didn't make the team that you said you'd
never try out for it again?"

Parents who wish to communicate with their adolescents
should first choose an appropriate time. A relaxed and effective dialogue is unlikely when the adolescent is rushing to
school or arriving home late from a date. If either party is
rushed, preoccupied, or angry, the conversation can and
should be postponed.

The parent who conveys interest and caring is usually
easy for his adolescent to approach. When a parent is not involved in his child's life, there is no reason for the child to discuss anything of meaning or value with him. It is ideal if close
family ties are established in early childhood and never
broken or frayed, but it is never too late to attempt to mend
them. However, for a parent to find a delicate balance between concern and overconcern is vitally important.

For both parents and teenagers, perhaps the most difficult aspect of intrafamily communication is effective listening. While conversing, frequently neither party listens but
only pauses while contemplating his retort. It is far more important that one consider the other's point before continuing
his platform. When either disagrees, he should hear the other
out without interrupting and with an open mind. He may

then attack the theory, but never the individual. It is also helpful at these times that a parent not "pull rank", insisting that since he is the parent, he is right. It is this kind of logic that turns teenagers away.

Complimenting the young person on particularly good points or ideas carefully considered encourages further communication. If an adolescent feels that at least some of his feelings and thoughts have merit in his parents' eyes, he will look forward to trying out other theories on them.

Productive communication often ceases when it turns into an advice-dispensing session. When advice is solicited it is sometimes desired, but even then the adolescent often only wants someone to explore alternatives with him. He seldom wants a decision made for him. Providing solutions typically puts the parent in a precarious spot—suppose his answer does not work? It is doubtful that he will be approached again. An interested, "What do you think?" or "Let's first discuss some of your feelings about this," is much more helpful. When a young person feels that he has made his own decision he is more apt to feel good both about himself and his parents for not attempting to impose their own wishes. The youngster is better able to learn from a decision he has reached on his own. When he reaches his own conclusion, a parental comment upon the wisdom of his choice will likely reinforce his confidence in his decision-making abilities.

Most adolescents do not appreciate parents adopting their slang or manner of talk anymore than they like seeing the older generation affect their apparel. Parents imitating their young has not been found to facilitate communication between parent and child. Instead of admiring these parents for being up-to-date, young people are more inclined to be embarrassed for them or to make fun of them for trying so hard to recapture their youth: "I never could talk to my father. We were from two different worlds. Then my dad started letting his hair grow long. This was soon followed by a beard and some really wild clothes. After he got himself together and learned a few 'in' words, he sat me down and said, 'Son, let's rap about this drug scene, man.' I think he got that line from a B movie about New York musicians made in the forties. I didn't know whether to laugh or to cry, but it was pitiful—really sad. I said, 'Man, it's too late now,' and walked out. I had tears in my eyes, and I'm still not really sure that I know why."

Sometimes one parent is hurt or feels excluded because his adolescent prefers consulting and communicating with the other parent. After discussing this with his marital partner, he may decide to take this matter up with their teenager. Usually such a situation is more easily handled by the parent first approached. He can casually bring in his spouse by saying, "Let's see how your mother feels about this," or, "Your father and I were discussing this ourselves. He had some good ideas, why not talk it over with him?"

Effective communication between adolescent and parent is really no different from relevant dialogue between any two people. Ideally this involves empathy, concern, creative listening, and no interruptions. There should be no advice giving, moralizing, or manipulation. Meaningful interaction between the two generations becomes more difficult because of defensiveness on one side and an attempt to control on the other. If each tries to look at the other not as a parent or as a child but as a concerned human being trying to relate to another, the path to real communication becomes smoother.

5 As Long as You're Under My Roof: Maintaining Discipline

Good parents do not always produce considerate, well-disciplined youngsters; nor do so-called "bad" parents necessarily breed delinquents. But what parents teach, both verbally and by example, strongly influences how their child adjusts to society.

Authority is an inescapable fact of life, and the acceptance of authority is a primary condition for harmonious relations among all people. A young person's attitude toward authority is primarily derived in infancy and usually evolves from his experience with limits set by his parents. Unfortunately, it is difficult for parents to impose the precise amount of restriction to insure that their child will grow up neither compulsive nor altogether lacking in impulse control.

Too much authority, whether it be harsh physical punishment, constant regimentation, or verbal abuse, may produce resentment, hostility, and/or strong guilt feelings in adolescents. On the other hand, too little setting of rules and limits may give a youngster an inflated sense of his own worth and little sensitivity to the needs and rights of others.

The overly disciplined child commonly finds outlets for his hostility through physical aggression or in theft, drug abuse, or another lifestyle calculated to bring shame upon his parents. If an adolescent does not learn to curb his own impulses and emotions he cannot become a responsible and sensitive human being. Since this is the goal of most parents

41

for their children, the importance of discipline cannot be over-emphasized. The methods of discipline are probably not half as crucial as is the spirit behind them. Parents should not impose authority simply to dominate, but to provide guidelines and to teach cooperation and self-reliance.

Each young person responds to authority in a different manner. Some passively accept limits and discipline; a minority actively resist. Still others find it a challenge to outwit or get around restrictions imposed by authority figures. Whether passive acceptance or active resistence is less healthy is a moot point. Neither attitudes toward authority are ones parents wish to instill in their youngsters.

Many parents encourage independence in their youngsters. Others foster dependency from their youngsters' earliest childhood—protecting them from both physical and psychological injury, keeping them forever at their sides and preventing any practice in decision making or the possibility of their getting hurt. These practices seriously interfere with the child's development of self-reliance and independent judgment.

Studies indicate that close-knit families seem to produce youngsters with more self-confidence and independence, as compared with loosely organized families. When parents have kept their children dependent, they later transfer this dependence to their peer group. Conversely, when children develop independence, they are better able to stand up against both adult and peer group pressures.

What often stymies parents is when their placid youngster seems to change so dramatically into an argumentative, hostile adolescent. "It is as if everything he had been taught throughout his life was examined, discarded and new reactions were mobilized immediately," a distraught mother of a sixteen-year-old boy lamented. "My word, which used to be respected, is now ignored or even ridiculed. 'What do you know?' he'll taunt. 'You're out of it. You have no right to set rules for me—you're in another generation.' I swear, this boy makes me feel stupid, inadequate—even antiquated. Then I hate myself for letting him get to me this way. He knows it hurts, but he enjoys it. This from a child who didn't give me a moment's worry until a few months ago. I don't know what to do or where to turn."

Young people who for whatever reason are unable to voice their frustrations and aggression toward their parents as authority figures may project these feelings to other authority figures such as teachers, policemen, employers or even to societal institutions, for example, the law, the military, the government. Some parents are surprised to find that their passive, agreeable, and compliant teenagers are "acting out" in school, becoming disciplinary problems, or even indulging in illegal acts as a means of venting their frustrations toward authoritarianism. Often youngsters behaving in this manner are model children at home; fearful of parental rejection and disapproval. They frequently come from rigid, patriarchal homes where authority is never questioned.

CASE HISTORY

"Elizabeth always did what she was told—that's why her behavior is so astonishing to us now. I guess her father and I were spoiled. She never questioned our authority until she started high school. She got into the wrong crowd, and I imagine that they taught her that lying to her parents was THE thing to do. She'll lie when it's easier to tell the truth. We heard from several of our friends that she had been seen with her gang at a rock concert smoking marijuana. We had been told that she was going to a movie and then spending the night with a friend. When we asked where she had been, she became belligerent and told us it was none of our business. We made her swear that she had been where she was supposed to be. We then sprang it on her that we knew all along she'd gone to that forbidden concert, and further, that she had been using drugs. We intimated that we'd hired a private detective to follow her so that we'd always know where she was.

"She became indignant and even screamed at us. She

accused us of not trusting her—her own parents! When we tried to tell her how much she was hurting us and how it was her friends we didn't trust, not her, she called us hypocrites. We don't know where we have failed, but as I told Elizabeth's father, I think it's that crowd she's been running around with."

Frequently parents are too involved with their own activities to properly supervise their youngsters. Many are afraid that they will look like interfering parents if they discipline when other parents do not. Parents often do not check to see if there will be adult supervision at a slumber party or other planned activity. Either they do not want to take the time or they cannot risk their adolescent's anger by calling another parent to see if approval has been obtained for their youngster's visit. Just so their adolescents stay out of trouble (or appear to do so) and do not become too much of a bother, they assume that they are fulfilling their roles as parents.

CASE HISTORY

Stacy: fifteen years: "All the kids tell me how lucky I am that my parents let me come in whenever I like, choose my own clothes, date who I want, and, well, do anything I'm big enough to do. I used to agree, but now I know that they simply don't care. I can't remember my mother ever asking me who I was going out with or anything except, 'Did you have a good time, dear?' in her faked caring voice. That's it exactly—she doesn't care. Oh, they'd care if I was arrested or addicted or something drastic that would cause them some time or embarrassment—but I personally think it's upsetting for both of them to have a kid my age and size. It's tough for my mother especially to play the young debutante type when a 5'9", 140-pound girl comes in the room and calls her Mom. When they have parties it's just like a role-reversal—they expect me to get lost and to stay away until everyone's gone.

"I stayed out all night and only got one question, 'Are you pregnant, Stacy?' It's a wonder I'm not. Charles and I have been together like that over six months. He's kind of domineering, but I need that. At least he cares, but I wish when he got mad at me for something he wouldn't get so physical. Most parents wouldn't let their fifteen-year-old daughter date a guy twenty years old. Mine don't care. One night when I came in with a black eye I prayed for them to notice but, of course, that was asking for too much. But don't blame Charles. He loves me—at least he shows that he cares."

Dislike, disrespect, and finally, disregard, characterize many young people's attitudes toward authority figures, whether they be parents, teachers, or The Law. Particularly when in groups, youngsters attempt to impress each other with their defiant attitudes and actions. When young people are disrespectful and/or unruly, adults must control this behavior and redirect it, while attempting to preserve the offender's dignity and self-respect. Public punishment and embarrassment defeat the self-discipline adults are trying to teach. In many instances, young people act with impudence and sarcasm toward adults because they are afraid to show their real feelings for fear of peer rejection. Adults are often mystified when adolescents act in a disrespectful manner for no apparent reason.

CASE HISTORY

Carole, an eighth grade student, disliked school primarily because much of it was difficult for her. She struggled to keep up, but in her more stringent academic subjects it was impossible. She further was apprehensive in the classroom: reciting was painful and explaining why the homework assignment was incomplete was traumatic. Carole had no friends among her classmates and she desperately craved their acceptance.

When she received extra help after school in her algebra class, Carole was quiet but extremely polite and grateful to the teacher for the tutoring. Therefore Mrs. M., her teacher, was shocked that Carole was rude and belligerent when asked the answer to a problem which she knew how to work. Carole said loudly, "I don't know—and no one cares! You just assign stuff so we'll be busy and you won't have to teach." Her remarks were greeted with laughs and applause from a few members of the class, so Carole was momentarily pleased with her retort. The teacher quietly explained that her comments were untrue and inappropriate. After class, Carole apologized to the teacher, since she sincerely realized that she was wrong. Carole was surprised and hurt that her classmates treated her no differently after her so-called success in algebra—she still was not included.

Many parents feel their adolescents are extremely impatient—they will consider postponing nothing; instantaneous gratification is demanded. Unless the parents continually "supply" they are castigated or ignored. Parents frequently complain that their young people want everything the other kids have, and many use all sorts of manipulative techniques to get their parents to yield.

Parents can usually expect that their youngsters will be more critical and rebellious when their friends are around. This is also the time they may ask for or demand special privileges that they know their parents would customarily deny. It is unfair for young people to put their parents in awkward situations, that is, asking in front of a friend if that friend could stay for dinner; telling parents that they were volunteered to take a group of kids to a game; or observing that the person spending the night has a later curfew. Confrontations of this nature demand a forthright response: "You're putting me in an uncomfortable position. I wish you had asked earlier if your friend could stay for dinner—I'd have planned for it." "Please don't volunteer us for anything until you've asked us first. Now it's your responsibility to phone your friends to tell them that you'll need to arrange another means of transportation to the game." "When your friends sleep at our home, they'll have to adopt our rules temporarily."

"Parents know best." "Because I'm your mother, that's why." "Because I said so, that's reason enough." "Because I'm the adult in this house." "Because." Statements of this nature create much hostility in the adolescent. They further do not teach that for every rule and limit set, there should be a legitimate reason. Adolescents feel such comments are made either to demonstrate who is in control or to cover for the fact that their parents do not have good reasons for their regulations.

Adolescents need rules that leave no room for interpretation. Parents should say, "It's all right to tell us how mad your little brother makes you, but you can't hit him." Teenagers have enough confusion in their young lives, so parental guidelines should not be subject to their misinterpretation. "If you want a dog, you must pay for his shots and be responsible for his feeding, training, and exercise," rather than: "Be sure to take care of your dog;" "You must do your homework before going to the game," instead of: "Remember, school work is most important." Parents need to refrain from becoming The Enemy. Although they will argue with the older generation's rationale and reasoning, most teenagers basically respect consistency and clarity, not innuendos and half-statements. Parents, however much they desire their young to be grateful for the many years of care and time devoted to them, should not expect to be thanked or appreciated for their efforts.

Often when families plan house rules and regulations together and the youngsters are allowed a voice in formulating policies, confrontations can be avoided. Family conferences may also be utilized when a member feels a policy change is in order. Adolescents and preadolescents report that deciding curfews, allowances, household tasks, and other policies as a family unit makes them feel more responsible and more apt to behave responsibly.

It is particularly helpful when both parents of an adolescent initially come to terms on the setting of limits and approaches to discipline. The united front that they present to their youngsters from early childhood may save them considerable trouble in the years to come. Most teenagers are quick to identify the more lenient parent: "Dad, Mom says no car for two weeks, but how about slipping me the keys before you leave tonight? You know how she is. She just flew off the handle for no reason and grounded me." Later, to friends: "The old lady found my third speeding ticket tonight and grounded me, but as usual old Dad came through. He'd fall for any line I'd give him."

Does this adolescent respect his father for always giving in? Does it make him love his father more? And what are the father's motives for needing to be the good guy? Is he trying to win his child's friendship or love? Is this undermining of his wife's authority a way of getting back at her?

Parents who have not maintained discipline with their youngsters from early childhood should not anticipate respect and obedience when their children reach their teens. Often browbeaten parents throw up their hands and give in. The adolescents are victorious in this power struggle and their parents declare defeat: "I can't make her do anything anymore. She threatens to run away if I do." "He said we're the reason he took drugs in the first place and if we didn't lay off the nagging he'd do it again." "She says it's her business if she engages in sex, and if we try to discipline her, she'll marry him." "She tells us if we don't let her smoke cigarettes, she'll smoke something stronger."

Those parents who let their youngsters live their own lives, since to impose restraints would be to risk dire consequences, are risking more than they can imagine—their adolescents' respect. It takes courage to maintain a firm "no" in the face of adolescent threats and ploys, but giving in is not winning in the long run. Parents cannot gain their youngsters' admiration or love by letting themselves be trampled on. Nor can bribery be effective for more than a brief period.

Many parents use threats in an attempt to control their youngsters' behavior. Not only is this technique usually ineffective, but it is often learned quickly by young people and used to manipulate their parents.

"The next time you come in at 2:00 A.M. *I'll* _____"; "If I catch you with him again, you're _____." "If I ever see you smoking again, I'll _____." Making threats and failing to carry through when the almost inevitable next time does happen may give youngsters the idea that their parents are big talkers and little doers. When threats are made, they must be carried out so that a credibility gap between parents' words and actions is not created in their youngster's eyes. (Of course, the mother who threatened, "If I ever catch you with a drink in your hands, I'll kill you!" should not feel obligated to keep her promise should her daughter partake.) When authority figures do not carry out their edicts, their words may fall on heedless ears.

Beset with problems, young personalities can certainly benefit from guidance. But parents should not feel slighted when youngsters go to people their parents perceive as "outsiders" with their problems, since adolescents are eager to free themselves from their childish parental dependency. Teenagers are frequently more receptive and responsive to outside guidance in the areas of decision making and discipline. Too frequently teenagers interpret parental intervention as interference. By parents not becoming hurt or upset by their lack of involvement in all of their adolescents' problems and concerns, many potential problems may be avoided.

Without exposure to discipline and limit-setting throughout their lives, adolescents cannot be expected to live successfully as adults in a societal structure demanding order and cooperation. Probably one of the most difficult tasks facing parents is achieving the right balance of restraint coupled with the appropriate degree of freedom and consistency necessary to produce well-adjusted adults.

6 Peers' Influence on Sexual Attitudes and Behavior

Sex is many things to the American adolescent: a source of physical pleasure, a means of communication, an object of curiosity, an index of maturity, an escape from loneliness, a means of rewarding or punishing others, and a response to peer group pressures, according to Sorensen.[1]

It is frequently young people's insecurity which causes them to so readily adopt others' ideas of morality or sexual standards. Too many are pitifully ill-equipped to stand alone and buck the crowd when it is so much easier to drift with it.

Ideally, an adolescent's sexual behavior is determined by his personal convictions rather than by what his group advocates. If young people know their own feelings and have been allowed to express these viewpoints as they mature, they will probably feel more comfortable expressing opinions in a setting comprised of their peers.

CASE HISTORY

Ellen, age fourteen: "I really didn't know what I was getting myself into. Of course, I knew some of the basics of sex—my mother took care of that. She gave me a weird book to read and told me if I had questions

---

[1]Robert C. Sorensen, *Adolescent Sexuality in Contemporary America.*

that she would try to answer them. But there was no way I'd discuss any of that with her. My girl friends and I had been joking about guys, our own physical development and things like that for a couple of years. Only this past year have I been allowed to date and you wouldn't believe my parents' warnings! It seems they automatically think any boy who asks me for a date wants only one thing—sex. And they obviously don't trust me—their threats and warnings are unbelievable. My mom stays up for me after dates and checks me out—looking me over carefully and quizzing me about the evening's activities. She seems particularly suspicious if I am even a few minutes late. My best friend and I used to laugh about our early curfews—as if you couldn't do the same things before eleven that you could afterwards!

"It's always been important to me to have friends and, I guess, to be popular. When my best friend told me that she wasn't a virgin it shocked me a little, I guess. I quickly assured her I felt that if you were in love anything was O.K. I guess it made her feel better. I found out that more and more of my friends were having sexual experiences—especially if they were going steady. When I started dating Allen he seemed to expect it after a few dates. We discussed it a lot; at first I really didn't want to. I know my parents would kill me if they found out—and I guess that morally, even now, I think that sex should be for after marriage. He didn't buy any of my arguments and he suggested that I talk it over with my girl friends. He probably knew most of them were doing it.

"Well, I really wanted to keep going with him and the girls assured me that he wouldn't be around long if I didn't—it would just be easier and more fun for him to date someone who did; so I gave in. I didn't really get anything out of it, but he seemed to and we dated three months before he suddenly quit loving me. That's when I really started feeling horrible . . . guilty.

My girl friends were great then. They stuck by me and helped fix me up with David. He's older—eighteen, in fact, and at first I thought my folks wouldn't approve. But they wanted me to be happy and popular so much that they let me date him. I was really surprised. Of course, he expected sex right away—and it was much easier for me with the second guy. I'm sure it will continue to be easier, too."

CASE HISTORY

Don, age seventeen: "Since I was one of the last in my class to mature physically, I was continually being teased by the other guys. My physical education class was almost more than I could stand. I didn't mind so much being kidded about being a baby, but when they began to hint about my lack of manliness, they knew they'd hit something that hurt. From then on I was called a fag, queer, homo—and then the girls heard the rumors. They, the girls, I mean, didn't give me a bad time; they just ignored me. My parents knew something was bothering me but I couldn't discuss it with them. The only adult who knew what I was going through was my coach and he thought the whole thing was funny. He even made a few remarks himself. I thought it might help if I dated, but I knew none of the girls my age would have anything to do with me. Finally I got a thirteen-year-old to go out with me. She was just in seventh grade but I told myself she looked older. We had a hard time even getting together since her parents thought she was too young to date. Now I feel terrible about what I did to her, but it's too late. She was dumb about sex, really knew even less than I did—and the second time we were together we went to bed. I didn't rape her but she couldn't stop me once I got started. I had the best feeling—I mean I guess

I realized then I really wasn't queer. I could have cared less about her. To make it even worse, I told several of my friends about it— to prove to them, you know, that I was all right. Now she's probably having to put up with some hard times from the kids—I don't know. I never want to see her again."

Times have changed radically and the influences today's adolescents are exposed to are very different from those their parents encountered. This factor makes communication about sex between these two generations complicated. An even greater obstacle appears to be lack of mutual trust between parents and teenagers. Sex is an intensely personal topic and a teenager will not share his feelings with a parent he does not respect or trust.

A major concern is reconciling the adolescent's physical maturity with his emotional immaturity. Often this early physical maturation coupled with peer approval motivates teenagers to early marriages. The high divorce rate of teen marriages indicates that most of these adolescents are not emotionally prepared for marriage or for being parents. Yet over half of all first-born babies in this country are born to mothers twenty-one years of age or younger. Pressure toward earlier social maturity from those significant in their young lives cannot help but promote sexual irresponsibility. Parents directing their youngsters' social lives, fearful that they might not be "popular," often concern themselves with this, rather than helping to develop responsible sexual standards and attitudes.

In the area of sex it is definitely the parents' responsibility to help their youngsters examine alternatives and consequences. It is further the parents' obligation to teach values, set limits, and provide positive examples. Couples who respect, love, and enjoy each other do much to create a positive image of sex and marriage in the minds of their youngsters.

Some parents feel that since most of the public and private schools presumably teach sex education, starting in the elementary grades and continuing throughout high school, their responsibility in this area is absolved. Nothing could be further from the truth. When sex education is in the curriculum, it is likely to be only factual in content, teaching nothing of the emotional and psychological factors involved when one engages in a sexual relationship; adolescents may be taught the "how's" of sex, but seldom, in a classroom setting, the "why's." Too, many educators have been assigned this topic who feel either ill-equipped or embarrassed to teach it, and their negative feelings are certainly communicated to perceptive youngsters. One teacher remarked that personally she felt sex should never be discussed in a mixed setting, but she was certain that none of her eighth grade students in the sex education class knew of her bias. Several students remarked that since they knew how humiliated and strait-laced she was, they spent much of their classtime thinking of what she would perceive as "dirty questions" to ask.

Many young people are, as the saying goes, "in love with love." Going with only one person gives some youngsters a feeling of security that may be lacking in their other relationships, and steady dating is usually looked on with favor by one's group. In fact, often adolescents report that their status within the crowd varies according to who they are dating and whether they are going steady. Their position drops significantly when they are dateless. Some girls report a feeling of desperation when they perceive themselves as undesirable to the opposite sex. One stated that the only way she finally became popular was to start some rumors about herself and then boys began taking her out to see if the word about her was legitimate. "I had to 'put out' to become popular, and if I had it to do over again I know that I'd do the same thing. It's better than loneliness and better than all the kids thinking something's wrong with you."

Dr. Haim Ginott contrasted romantic with mature love: "In mature love, neither boy nor girl tries to exploit or possess the other. Each belongs to himself. Such love gives the

"*The Board of Education requires me to give you some basic information on sex, reproduction and other disgusting filth.*"

freedom to unfold and to become one's best self."[2] This definition may be extremely helpful to a young person's question: "Is this the real thing?" Ginott wrote that romantic love is often blind—acknowledging strength and not seeing weakness in the love object. This "romantic" version of love—possessive, blind, and/or exploitive unfortunately cannot be said to be peculiar to adolescents. This is the "love" most often depicted in movies, fiction, television, and too frequently, by the parents of today's adolescents.

Studies indicate that from fifty to eighty percent of America's adolescents are engaging in premarital sex. Parents, educators, and concerned adults must help these young people and those who follow to understand their bodies, their responsibilities to themselves, and their responsibilities to their sexual partners. Many engaged in research in adolescent sexuality hypothesize that responsibility to each other will not be a significant variable in relationships that young people will prefer in the future. This is an unfortunate commentary and we tend to support the opposite viewpoint. We feel that engaging in sexual experiences without a sense of responsibility toward one's partner may initially appeal to the immature adolescent, but eventually will prove empty and meaningless.

What seems unusual is that many adolescents engaging in sex say that they do not really enjoy it. They regard it more as something that is expected—a duty, an obligation. The attitude that sex is inevitable, shared by many of their peers, pressures both male and female adolescents into premature sexual experimentation.

There is a trend among adolescents away from the age-old double standard that premarital sex is acceptable for males, but not for females. It appears that most young people are tolerant and open toward premarital sex for both sexes. Many adolescents are attempting to be more honest in their sexual relationships and the majority appear to feel that a personal moral code is essential.

---

[2] Haim G. Ginott, *Between Parent and Teenager*, pp. 175-76

When parents initially discover that their adolescents have been sexually involved, many react first with panic and then with anger. Although it is extremely difficult for most to remain calm under these circumstances, little productive communication can take place in a shouting match.

Inflicting guilt is rarely beneficial. Parents who blame their youngster (How could you do this to us?), his friends (They got him into this!) or those who chastise themselves (Where did we fail?) should be considering solutions instead. Sometimes parents find that rational, unemotional, and productive discussion about sexual matters with their adolescent is impossible. If this is the case, then every attempt should be made to find a responsible adult with whom the youngster can communicate, since what he most likely will be getting from his peers is their unqualified and unanimous support.

Many teenagers' knowledge of sex is faulty and some of their misconceptions are astounding:

"You can't get pregnant the first time you have intercourse."

"Once you have VD, you'll never get it again."

"If withdrawal is practiced, you can't get pregnant."

"You're safe for one night if you can get a birth control pill."

"Masturbation causes sterility."

"_____ (fill in any contraceptive method here) is one hundred percent effective."

Some attitudes that convey sexual irresponsibility are alarming:

"If she gets pregnant, that's her bad luck. I wasn't the first guy who had her."

"If I get pregnant, I know I can make him marry me."

"If you get pregnant, you can always get an abortion."

"Sex is all right for boys before marriage—but not for girls."

"Since VD is easily treated, I'm not that worried about getting it."

"There's no way I'd tell a doctor who I've had sex with.

How embarrassing if my friends found out they might have contracted VD from me."

For numerous reasons, including changing sexual mores, venereal disease has reached epidemic proportions in this country, despite increased public attention devoted to the problem. In days past, VD was seldom discussed, but since gonorrhea and syphilis are two of the most prevalent communicable diseases in the nation, this topic can no longer be ignored.

Many young people are hesitant, embarrassed, or afraid to talk with their parents about VD, so when a youngster suspects that he may have such a disease he often consults with his close friends and takes their all too limited or faulty advice. Often adolescents reassure their friends that their symptoms will disappear, or worse, they suggest self-treatment—and some of the peer group's "home remedies" have been known to range from aspirin to listerine.

Recent medical evidence indicates that the pill may cause physiological changes, making a female more susceptible to gonorrhea and fungus infections. Since females rarely notice any symptoms of gonorrhea initially, the implications of increased use of the pill are overwhelming.

Parents of adolescents and preadolescents need to know the facts about venereal diseases, but, more importantly, must be able to impart this information to their youngsters. If they feel unable to discuss this topic with their children, they should provide them with up-to-date literature on VD, its symptoms and its cures. The ultimate solution to venereal disease is education. If treated soon enough, both syphilis and gonorrhea can be quickly and rather painlessly cured. The majority of health departments now have public clinics where treatment is free and confidentiality assured. Increasingly, states are passing laws permitting treatment of teenagers without involving their parents.

Most young people report that they feel group sex is one activity in which they would never engage. Those interviewed who had experienced group sex expressed their reluctance to participate in at least their initial experience. Several cliques were found that included within their initiation rites the provision that a novice be sexually intimate with all members. No matter how many previous sexual experiences a young person has had, many agree that sex in a group setting seems degrading and is usually more of a performance than an experience. Young people say that participants are frequently observing and commenting on each other's behaviors and that they feel their current partners are comparing them with the rest.

What often is not at the onset a sex party is apt to become one if drugs are plentiful, and they too frequently are. Often teenagers tell of participating in unorthodox sexual relations while using drugs, a pursuit that they would not have considered when "straight." It seems that many find it more difficult to resist manipulative techniques when under the influence of drugs and there is no doubt that some drugs make adolescents less inhibited and more suggestible.

CASE HISTORY

Kelly, age fifteen: "There are several requirements for initiation into the Rebels—that's the really exclusive almost nonsocial club at our school. By nonsocial, I mean we don't consider any cheerleader or class officer types—they're not real. The hardest thing for most of the sophomore girls is the rule that you have to have sex with all of the boys in the group, not just once, but any time they want you. Some of them have special girls and they don't do it, but most of them do. The older girls reassure us and tell us it's not so bad —that you get used to it. Besides that, by the time you're a junior or a senior the boys all like the freshmen or sophomores anyway. But right now if the older girls weren't helping me and telling me it's all right, I don't know what I'd do. I can't help but feel sick inside and I wish I'd never been asked to join in the first place. I guess if I had any guts, or any friends on the outside, I'd quit. But I don't anymore."

It is surprising to discover that many rapes are gang rapes, involving two or more men or boys assaulting one female. This is an example of peer pressure and male bonding, and "proof of a desire to humiliate the victim beyond the act of rape through the process of anonymous mass assault."[3] There is usually a leader whose prestige is maintained in his group by demonstrating his masculinity and his perception of femininity as merely a sexual tool.

Opinions regarding the effects of pornography on youth are diverse; one viewpoint charging that it leads to deviant sexual behavior and/or criminal behavior—particularly sexual crimes. Opposing opinion views obscene materials as a valuable method of discharging frustrated needs and providing a healthy sexual-fantasy outlet. Studies with adults adequate to validate either of these extremes are lacking, and studies with preadolescents or adolescents are almost nonexistent. It does seem reasonable to assume that the sexual confusion accompanying puberty, coupled with pornographic literature and films, could be extremely traumatic to a young person.

If these materials were actually unavailable to minors one could make the argument that what adults wish to view is their privilege. In actuality, however, many young people frequent "adult" book stores and "porno flicks," and emerge with even more feelings of turmoil, inadequacy, and confusion. Several have related that after being exposed to what may be termed hard-core pornography, they have felt that sexual behavior is "nauseating," "dirty," or "sick." Those already confused with sexual identity have seen homosexuality and bisexuality portrayed so attractively that heterosexuality seems a poor alternative.

Here, too, the peer group enters in: If a young person re-

---

[3]Susan Brownmiller, *Against Their Will: Men, Women, and Rape,* p. 187.

fuses to involve himself with pornographic materials, he may be labeled as immature and many cannot withstand this. It is easier to expose themselves to obscene films or pictures than to risk the humiliation of being ostracized or thought of as less than sophisticated.

More and more youngsters are opting for single parenthood when finding themselves pregnant, since they are viewing the viability of "have to" marriages with skepticism.

Only recently has the concept of an unmarried adolescent's keeping her child become popular and the peer groups' influence has been the deciding factor in numerous instances. The other girls in her crowd may tell a pregnant friend what fun they will all have, dressing and undressing the baby, taking turns babysitting, carrying it in their backpacks, and even what a hassle it will present to her parents: "Can't you just see your mother's face when you tell her you're keeping the kid? There'll be no way she can hide it. Even her bridge club will know!" With such support and encouragement, an adolescent may be much more inclined to upset and disappoint her parents rather than her friends. She has probably been the star of her social set during her pregnancy; a reversal of the peer censure she would have received a few years before.

Some keep their babies as a sheer defiance of authority, while other young girls reveal that the women's movement which deemphasizes the importance of men was the deciding factor for them. Still others say they feel there is almost a stigma attached to giving up a child for adoption now.

The fact is that illegitimate births have more than tripled in the last twenty years, and they now account for one out of eight births. Numerous social workers reveal that although they have no statistics to substantiate their claim, they sense an increasing number of child abuse cases among young unwed mothers. If this is so, it is probably because few youngsters are emotionally prepared for the rigors of childrearing.

Population experts say that despite the new sexual freedom, sexually active teenagers are still reluctant to use contraceptives. Many hypothesize that using a contraceptive device takes the spontaneity out of sex, implying premeditation and planning, which some young women do not wish to admit. to. Other girls perceive contraceptives as bothersome or harmful. Also, some young women consciously or subconsciously want to get pregnant.

Many parents, for religious, personal, or moral reasons, do not want their daughters to undergo abortions. Their daughters may have even stronger convictions about abortions. Most parents would not wish their underaged, unmarried daughters to attempt to rear a child born out of wedlock. They realize how poorly equipped their adolescents are to be parents and further suspect that they, the parents, will end up being responsible for the infants after the newness wears off. If the decision is made that the pregnancy will not be terminated, it is often advisable for an adolescent to complete her pregnancy either at a special boarding school or with out-of-town friends or relatives. This is usually easier and saves embarrassment for both the young woman and her parents. It further removes her from peer guidance which may not be in her best interest.

When parents insist that their daughter "marry the boy who's responsible so the child will have a father," they are usually asking for trouble. Beginning a marriage while in one's teens is usually arduous enough without adding the responsibility of a child before the couple has had time to adjust to each other. This is more than most teenage marriages can tolerate. It is exceptional when such a forced marriage is successful.

When an unmarried adolescent becomes pregnant, no matter how the situation is handled, counseling is usually beneficial. Frequently the adolescent feels that the wrong decision was made regarding her situation. A concerned adult may help her to sort through these mixed emotions, accept her decision, and plan realistically for her future.

Much controversy surrounds the issue of whether a minor should have her parents' permission in order to obtain birth control supplies. Some physicians will only prescribe birth control pills with parental permission, while others feel that this matter is purely between them and their patients and prescribe when they see a need. Several states have recently passed laws giving minors the right to seek medical services and prescription drugs from a physician without parental knowledge or consent. In some states a minor may be able to seek psychiatric or psychological services, again with confidentiality being insured. This typically happens within an agency rather than in a private setting.

If an adolescent girl chooses to discuss birth control with her parents and asks their permission for obtaining a prescription for the pill, they have been afforded a unique opportunity to discover what factors are influencing her decision to engage in premarital sex. They can find out if she is really just going along with the crowd, discover why she feels sexual intimacy is necessary in her particular relationship, determine her regard for her partner, and, hopefully, help her to analyze her own feelings regarding herself and her sexuality.

Due to more liberal laws in this area, abortions are becoming less expensive, legal, and generally easier to obtain. Counsel both before and after the abortion should be required but, unfortunately, often is neglected or is superficial at best. Additional counselor training in this field is sorely needed.

Whereas many adolescent girls, as well as adult women, are able to undergo abortions without any obvious psychological side effects, others are vulnerable at any age. Studies do not correlate this guilt or trauma with any particular religious orientation or family childrearing practices; so it may be inferred that the psychological makeup of each individual woman is the prevailing variable.

Adult women have related that an abortion they obtained years before still interferes with their emotional wellbeing and sexual functioning. Young and seemingly liberal adolescent girls have reported that they have felt unworthy and "numb" when they opted for an abortion—particularly when they were coerced by their family to make this decision. One girl of eighteen stated: "Since my abortion, I have been totally unresponsive sexually. Even though I have taken every precaution to protect myself against pregnancy, I still count the days each month—knowing I'm pregnant. I don't enjoy sex anymore. I just go through the motions to reassure myself of my desirability or something. I guess a shrink could tell me why I persist in this promiscuous manner. I'm sure not getting anything out of it."

Abortion appears to be the preferable alternative for many young pregnant women. They prefer this to months of pregnancy, trying to make awesome decisions regarding keeping the baby or giving the child up for adoption; marrying or staying single; giving up educational plans or trying to pursue them. Several have said that abortion was their choice because their reputations were protected.

When a young woman thinks she is pregnant, often the last people in the world she considers telling are her parents. Studies frequently indicate that most tell their close peers, but many tell no one until it is too late to consider all alternatives available. Often a pregnant teenager's parents appear more concerned about the pregnancy than about their youngster's attitudes and feelings, and unfortunately, many adolescents believe that their parents' real concern is what their neighbors or friends will think.

According to Dr. Bennett Olshaker, a psychiatrist, "One of the most disheartening aspects of the current attitude toward sexual behavior is that sex seems to be increasingly separated from intimacy. What was once in the realm of private pleasure has entered the area of public performance. We do not know what the eventual consequences will be relative to the sexual conduct of human beings. We can hope, however, that whether sex is premarital or marital, the involved partners will have regard for each other as people and not as objects."[4]

Romanticism has been supplanted by eroticism, and many adults feel that this philosophy has invaded every aspect of their adolescents' lives—from their music, movies, and literature to their dancing, lifestyles, and particularly their

---

[4]Bennett Olshaker, *What Should We Tell the Kids?* pp. 245-46.

new morality. A definition of eroticism is: pleasure without responsibility. The novelist J. B. Priestley called it "concentrating upon a certain kind of excitement and pleasure, to the exclusion of everything else."[5] This philosophy scorns love and sentiment, since these emotions entail involvement, commitment, and caring. A casual sexual encounter is permissible, however, since no deep feelings are attached.

Young people need to learn that sex at its best cannot be separated from commitment and intense caring. They also should realize that emotional strength helps one control his sexual drives and impulses. Sex, to be truly meaningful, must be shared by two mature, responsible, and loving partners. Few adolescents meet these basic requirements.

---

[5]Quoted in Harriet Van Horne, " 'Being in Love' Versus 'Having a Relationship,' " *Family Weekly*, November 2, 1975, p. 5.

7 Communes, Group Marriages, Homosexual Relationships, and Other Alternative Lifestyles

Young people, as well as many not so young, stream to communes for a number of reasons. Probably most significant is the need for a strong "family" feeling, or sense of belonging to a close-knit group. Over the past decade the communal movement has mushroomed at an explosive rate and there is no doubt that already some of our traditions, institutions, and values are reflecting this impact.

Communal living is generally endorsed by the adolescent's peers because it is "honest." Followers find it a preferable alternative to living under parental domination with "parents who are materialistic hypocrites, who have screwed up society and expect us to follow in their footsteps."

Dr. Herbert Otto, chairman of the National Center for the Exploration of Human Potential, La Jolla, California, visited numerous communes in various parts of the country. He observed that certainly the tribal movement is no longer exclusive to the so-called "hippie" or dropout—many are filled with exbusinessmen, professionals, and professors, often in their midtwenties or even older. Most communes share certain viewpoints, although each practices these to a greater or lesser extent. "Almost without exception, there is a deep respect and reverence for nature and the ecological system. There is clear awareness that seventy percent of the population lives on one percent of the land, that this one percent is severely polluted, depressingly ugly, and psychologically overcrowded."[1] The antiestablishment sentiment is widespread, and this naturally attracts the younger person searching for a group with which to unite against a common cause. Communal groups differ in how social change is to be effected; some wish to work within the system, others to set a humane example to the outside world, and, of course, the radicals prefer revolutionary tactics. Many of the young people interviewed who had shared communal experiences felt that they had made great strides in learning to relate with others openly and honestly, and most further believed they had become far less materialistic as a result of their experiences. Adolescents today are interested in mystic philosophies, unorthodox religions, the occult, astrology, yoga, or various forms of meditation, particularly those who are attracted to communal settings. Certainly pressure from those who "believe" is exerted so that the uninitiated can find new meaning in their lives. It has been observed that much switching from philosophy to philosophy goes on, and few real "truths" are discovered.

Although most communes insist that life can be joyous and beautiful when one is allowed to do that which he enjoys doing and does well, in practice this is all too frequently unfeasible. An oversimplified example: Four women who live in a communal situation enjoy sewing and knitting. None of these women or the men who live with them like cooking, housework, cleanup, or repairs—so who is to handle these matters? Realistically, in a commune, as in most home situations, one has certain unpleasant jobs and responsibilities which nonetheless must be done.

CASE HISTORY

After graduation from high school, Sue decided to join a commune for a brief period before entering college

---

[1]Herbert A. Otto, "Communes: The Alternative Life-Style," p. 17, *Saturday Review*, April 24, 1971.

in the fall. Needless to say, her parents were less than enthusiastic, but since Sue was no longer a minor, they could do nothing but wish her the best. She did promise them not to give up her educational plans.

Sue told of her initial enjoyment of the experiment in living: "Three girls and six boys share all of the chores. All of us work in the garden, but since none have a salable talent and none work outside of the commune, we are not self-sustaining. I write my parents and they send small checks to me every couple of weeks. However, the other kids' parents refuse all pleas for financial aid, so I guess we all depend on my folks. I hated to tell the others I was leaving in September; when I even broached the subject, they really applied the pressure. You know, 'We're your family now. You can't desert us.' I didn't have the heart to let them down. And that was a year ago. It's hard to believe that it's September again."

Probably more communes fail from lack of finances than for any other reason. Parents should not feel obligated to support young people who run away or join communes. Many communes survive from the money brought to them by young people who are asked or coerced to seek parental financial support. While it is difficult for parents to turn their backs on their children if they feel they are undernourished, poorly housed, or ill, there is always the alternative of returning home and living within the family guidelines.

Although many communes strongly resist formal, organized structure in any sense, almost invariably it will evolve along with a father and/or mother figure to make decisions for the group. Tribal jealousies, squabbles, and splits often ensue and members frequently leave to begin their own communal families. There is a great mobility and turnover in most communes.

After a communal living arrangement is abandoned, many young people have voiced confusion and concern over their past, more particularly the females. They question whether they will be able to settle down with one man or if any man will even want them. Others have experienced strong guilt feelings over past sexual behavior, particularly those reared in sheltered home situations; they may feel unworthy of ever becoming wives and/or mothers. Often motherhood has been the impetus to leave the commune, according to several adolescents. "I've messed up my life, but I have no right to further mess up my child's life." The majority of minors lack the judgment and maturity to live in a communal environment without suffering some ill effects.

A casualty often overlooked is the child born into a commune. Often all of the women are responsible for care of the children, and even the natural mother may have no idea who fathered the infant. These children may receive much love and attention, but they will lack strong familial attachments and parental models that children reared in traditional families receive.

Visitors who go to communes come far more often as voyeurs and thrillseekers, rather than to understand and to learn about this contemporary lifestyle. On the part of observers and reporters, curiosity primarily revolves around sleeping arrangements: "Do you sleep with the same person all of the time?" "Is group sex practiced in your commune?" "Is there some sexual initiation rite?" There is certainly a higher degree of sexual permissiveness in most of these societies when compared with more traditional lifestyles. But even here each commune differs. In some both heterosexuality and homosexuality are practiced by members; in others several couples relate sexually in various combinations; and in a very few, group sex is the rule. Increasing numbers of members in more recently established communes unite with one person in an intense, long-term relationship, much like a marriage.

Otto observed that a major problem in most communes is overcrowding and a lack of privacy.[2] Another concern is

---

[2]Otto, "Communes: The Alternative Life-Style," p. 20, *Saturday Review,* April 24, 1971.

establishing good community relations and this can be almost impossible in many cases, due probably to pressures exerted from the bad press many have received. Thus many communes are doomed before they become workable.

Peers very strongly influence whether a young person will consider attempting communal living. Those young people who are friendless, feel inadequate, unloved, and insecure are easily persuaded to be a part of any group that will accept them. They may well find themselves involved in movements contrary to their personal beliefs or in situations at variance with their convictions and values. These adolescents are likely to be recruited by a communal leader who not only has charisma, but also knows what tactics appeal to each potential family member.

Certainly the most sensational and widely publicized radical commune was one headed by the infamous Charles Manson, and his almost hypnotic control of its members should be considered. There has been much speculation about the methods he used to gain control of his followers.

Of the hundreds or possibly thousands that Manson met and attempted to entice to join with him, only a particular type chose to follow him. Almost every member of the family had dropped out, and most of them were found to have had a strong hostility toward society long before they joined Manson. "Those who chose to go with him did so, Dr. Joel Hochman testified, for reasons 'which lie within the individuals themselves.' In short, there was a need, and Manson seemed to fulfill it. But it was a double process of selection. For Manson decided who stayed. Obviously he did not want anyone who he felt would challenge his authority, cause dissention in the group, or question his dogma. They chose, and Manson chose, and the result was the Family. Those who gravitated to the Spahn Ranch and stayed did so because basically they thought and felt alike. This was his raw material."[3]

As Bugliosi and Gentry, coauthors of *Helter Skelter* ob-

---

[3]Vincent Bugliosi and Curt Gentry, *Helter Skelter*, p. 482.

served, Manson sensed and capitalized on his followers' needs. They doubted that he had magical powers, but felt he knew those who gravitated to him were searching for something. He merely discovered what it was and attempted to supply the need—be it a father figure, a Christ figure, or acceptance, love, and so on. He also introduced drugs to make his followers more suggestible; he used repetition, and with it erased inhibitions; he used isolation, sex, love, and fear. He also capitalized upon and developed in his followers their latent hatreds and focused them on the common enemy—the Establishment. He used religion, often indicating that he was the Second Coming of Jesus; he used music, which he knew reached young people; and he also used his unique experiences and his superior intelligence to manipulate others. He taught that life is a game (defiance of society), and that since everything is right, then nothing can be wrong.

There is more to Manson's charisma and power than professionals have been able to isolate and certainly further research is needed to analyze this particular personality type. Bugliosi and Gentry suggest that "whenever people unquestioningly turn over their minds to authoritarian figures to do with as they please—whether it be in a satanic cult or some of the more fanatic offshoots of the Jesus Movement, in the right wing or the far left, or in the mind-bending cults of the new sensitivity—those potentials exist. One hopes that none of these groups will spawn other Charles Mansons. But it would be naive to suggest that the chilling possibility does not exist."[4]

An extremely complex phenomenon is the middle-to-upper class, apparently well-adjusted youngsters' caravan to the communes. These preadolescents and teens often reject their parents and all that their generation represents. This makes them easy prey for a commune structured toward undermining and hassling authority figures.

Drugs are probably used to a slightly greater extent

---

[4]Bugliosi and Gentry, *Helter Skelter*, p. 485.

within communes, although some groups are totally opposed even to experimentation with drugs, including alcohol, and will expel violators. Many communes are characterized by a lack of energy and vitality which may be due in part to drug usage, but family members often admit that they just generally lack motivation. Others perceive ambition as an "Establishment hang-up" and purposely reject it, along with most values their parents attempted to teach.

Our country's latest vocal minority—the homosexuals—are estimated conservatively at about six million people. Young as well as older homosexuals are being pressured by their peers to "come out," a move that certainly will have a great impact on their lives. Since society's attitudes are moving toward greater acceptance, homosexuals have less to fear regarding discovery, although they still will probably be subjected to a great deal of rejection in various aspects of their lives.

The goal of most homosexual communes is to provide individuals who share a common way of life an opportunity to live and communicate together, united as a group, and to profit from the economy of the living situation. There are two strong views of homosexuality. One position is that homosexual behavior is not intrinsically abnormal and that it develops and is perpetuated much in the same way as is heterosexual behavior. The proponents of this theory feel that the homosexual is labeled abnormal because of society's prejudices. Therapists, however, have traditionally worked to help homosexuals to heterosexual orientations. Certainly prejudice still exists, and homosexuals must bear the heavy burden of discrimination, frequently coupled with guilt and self-hate.

Preadolescents and adolescents often have close relationships with those of the same sex, and these associations should be encouraged. Such friendships help to prepare them for intense relationships and sharing in their later lives. When they are warned that they are spending too much time with such a friend, or teased because their friends are of the same sex, they may be made to feel unnatural.

CASE HISTORY

Sharon and Charlotte had been friends in high school, and they happened to pledge the same sorority in college. After they were initiated, they chose to be roommates. Although both young ladies were well-liked, they dated rarely. They seemed to prefer school and sorority activities and both studied a great deal. Rumors developed about the girls and they were called in by the housemother for a discussion about their "unnatural" relationship. They were both mortified and angry, and Sharon soon quit school rather than to face the other girls in her sorority house, who all knew of the incident. Charlotte remained, but was socially ostracized and began to doubt her heterosexual orientation. She became frightened and disturbed and avoided any display of affection for members of her own sex.

It is unfortunate to hear of instances where young men have become worried because they have not wanted to engage in what they believed to be promiscuous behavior. Some feel that they must prove to their peers that they are not homosexual by engaging in sexual conquests.

In homosexual activities, "the peer group actually serves as a school of induction for some of its members. The uninitiated boy goes with one or more members of his peer group for indoctrination and his first experience."[5] Many young boys are socialized by their peer group in their first experiences in hustling homosexuals for the purpose of monetary gain. Sexual gratification is not a prime consideration in these relationships. These boys learn from their friends how and where to make contacts, the methods of securing money, and what behaviors are to be tolerated or rejected.

The "easy money" aspect through a sexual transaction

---

[5]Donald R. Cressey and David A. Ward, *Delinquency, Crime, and the Social Process*, p. 996.

with a homosexual, coupled with the conclusion that fewer risks are taken than those encountered in mugging or burglarizing makes this a not uncommon practice among delinquent teenage gangs. Certainly many boys whose peers sanction this practice reject homosexual transactions, but if they are to maintain status within their group they must conform in almost all other regards.

Multilateral marriages have not been studied until recently. Probably more are operating than are reported, because there exists a strong cultural taboo against such arrangements. Larry and Jean Constantine, behavioral scientists studying group marriages, report that the failure rate is better than one out of two. They felt that group marriage can be equated to a marathon that does not end—it takes a real commitment to genuine, substantial, and unrelenting personal growth to really make it function and work. In all of their research, they found only one commune practicing group marriage; these unions usually involve independent families.[6]

Frequently young people make disparaging remarks about the nuclear family. Some feel the monogamous family is totally lacking in meeting the needs of all persons involved. The principles of loyalty, fidelity, and commitment are considered outdated. They suggest that the conventional family is isolated, so an extension of the family, perhaps involving small monogamous groups, would be more meaningful. Advocates feel that close exposure to other couples is stimulating to both marital partners and that children profit from relating to more than two parent figures. They tend to disregard ensuing jealousies and guilt feelings that may evolve, as well as the dividing of authority over children and the resulting confusion when there are multiple parent-figures.

It is the rare adolescent who has sufficient judgment or

---

[6]Larry L. Constantine and Joan M. Constantine, *Group Marriage*, pp. 122–28. Copyright © 1973 by Larry L. Constantine and Joan M. Constantine.

maturity to join any movement to fulfill himself or herself through an extension of familial togetherness. This is most frequently used as the rationale for such a move, however. A good parental counter would be to suggest that their teenager first establish this openness, growth, and awareness within the boundaries of his own family.

Our country is organized around the couple, and too many seek marriage for that reason alone. Of course the "singles" have been rebelling against this tradition, with their own bars, parties, apartments, tours, and so on. Marriage is still preferred by the majority and probably will be for some time, although many agree that the traditional concept of marriage inhibits the individual growth and development of each partner.

While women were uneducated, dependent, and had no control over childbirth, they certainly could not hope for equality in all areas with men. In these circumstances husbands were saddled with full support for their wives and families, not only financially, but often emotionally and intellectually. Now that women have a choice about childbirth, they are afforded greater flexibility in areas such as education, social and professional rights, economic independence and a strong voice in decisions affecting their lives. Many young women are providing emotional support to their peers, helping them to overcome their anxieties and feelings of inadequacy that keep them from directly and effectively going after what they want with friends, relatives, and "authority figures." As a result sexual stereotypes are disappearing and couples should be more able to appreciate each other's identities. In the respect that the women's movement has done much to accelerate the emergence of equality, the so-called liberated woman who has worked to change her status but has not actively participated in the more radical aspects of the movement may be made to feel guilty. It is generally recognized that the women's movement at its most militant peak has been necessary to facilitate any change at all, but women who have created their emancipated identities are equally helpful by their own examples, and they are not so intimidating to the general public.

It is natural that many young people are discouraged with the concept of marriage, since they have watched their parents manipulate, frustrate, dominate, restrict, and stifle each other. They certainly do not want to get caught in the same trap.

CASE HISTORY

"My marriage is too confining," said Laura, a nineteen-year-old wife of one year. "I guess I expected that I'd still have a life of my own." Laura married Ted after she had completed one year of college. Ted, three years her senior, had been working to pay for a few hours of night school each semester. Both agreed that they could only afford tuition for one, and Laura suggested that she would be willing to support them financially while Ted finished his schooling. "Ted expects too much. I work hard and long hours as a bank teller—a job I hate—and he still expects me to do all of the shopping, cooking, and management of the apartment. He not only gets to go to school, but goes out with his friends several nights a week—to study, he says. They usually end up at someone's house or a bar, having a drink or just a good time. When I ask to go along, he pulls the old 'study bit,'and if I suggest doing something myself, he forbids it. He's terribly jealous and possessive; I'm smothered and unappreciated."

Most successful marriages provide both relatedness and freedom for each partner. Nena and George O'Neill describe the ideal marriage as "an honest and open relationship between two people, based on the equal freedom and identity of both partners. It involves a verbal, intellectual and emotional commitment to the right of each to grow as an individual within the marriage."[7] Many young people who marry with this philosophy feel that their relationship thrives because, being based on mutual caring and trust, it allows each enough freedom to remain an individual and to bring new strength and vitality to the union.

---

[7]Nena O'Neill and George O'Neill, *Open Marriage: A New Life Style for Couples,* p. 31. Copyright © 1972 by Nena O'Neill and George O'Neill. Reprinted by permission of the publisher, M. Evans & Co., Inc.

8 The Adolescent Escapists: Dropouts and Runaways

Adolescence is a time for learning, and this learning is not solely intellectual; emotional and social adjustments are the background against which all other skills are judged. An informal but democratic atmosphere within the schools seems to promote more willing acceptance of responsibility and more confident and competent adolescents. Young people schooled in nurturant conditions further demonstrate a higher degree of intellectual curiosity and initiative than students from traditional educational settings exhibit. Schools where unwarranted and excessive penalties are no longer attached to defeats promote students' happiness and feelings of success; factors which are directly connected to their continuance of school.

Statistics indicate the severity of the problem of the school dropout in our society; at present in the United States one out of every three fifth graders does not graduate from high school, although close to ninety percent of the youngsters will begin high school. Current research indicates that the present dropout rate in the United States is about thirty-five percent.

It is difficult to identify a potential dropout, although there is one causative factor that stands out in almost every study: Dropouts are loners who are much more dissatisfied with their peer relationships in school than are the high school graduates. They frequently reject self and school and usually feel unsure about their school status. In addition, the dropout is less respected than his classmates by his teachers, often expresses hostility toward authority figures, and does not appear to have well-defined goals. Research suggests that at high school age, thirty percent of the suicides occur among dropouts.

Beelick's study of sources of student satisfaction and dissatisfaction[1] suggests that the major sources of student satisfaction with school are achievement, recognition, the school work itself, and school activities. The major sources of dissatisfaction are the teacher's behavior, school policy, and administration, and interpersonal relations with peers. Satisfaction and dissatisfaction with school are found to have bearing on scholastic performance, personal ties, health, attitudes toward school, and the educational goals of a number of students.

This study has many implications: If the school were to provide more opportunities for achievement and recognition, if the work were more meaningful and relevant, the teachers screened to determine if they should or should not be in the classroom, and the policies or dictates of the administration revised; perhaps with student participation, more youngsters would stay in school. However, since the peer relationship still is a variable in determining satisfaction vs. dissatisfaction with school, is this a tangible that school personnel feels itself unable to affect? When discussing this situation with countless educators, one is likely to draw the following responses: "I can teach him grammar, but I can't teach him how to be liked." "My job is not to teach acceptance—but math." "That's not my problem, it's the counselor's." "Maintaining discipline alone is a full-time job." "You can't expect me to help the others to like him. I can't stand him myself." "Popularity isn't important. We need to look at true values."

A perceptive and knowledgeable teacher who truly cares about his students can do much to increase understanding

---

[1]Delbert B. Beelick, "Sources of Student Satisfaction and Dissatisfaction." p. 22, *Journal of Educational Research,* Sept. 1973.

and to create an atmosphere of togetherness in the classroom which will facilitate peer interaction and acceptance. Those who do not perceive the peer group as having tremendous influence on both students' behaviors and their emotional development probably have no business being in the classroom in the first place.

Brookover and his associates studied the relationship of self-concept of ability to school achievement. They defined "self-concept of ability" as "those definitions a student holds of his ability to achieve in academic tasks as compared to others."[2] Brookover hypothesized that among potentially successful students academic achievement is artificially limited by the child's self-concept of his ability to achieve. He believes that this low self-concept is a result of perceived negative evaluations of significant others. His research indicates that self-concept of ability functions independently of measured intelligence in influencing academic achievement and is a better predictor of academic achievement. Brookover found that positive changes in evaluations by significant others will raise the child's self-concept of ability and positively influence academic achievement. It is valid to speculate that if the above-mentioned positive changes by significant others do, in fact, raise self-esteem, self-concept of ability and academic achievement, they would also be a significant factor in keeping adolescents in school.

Deutsch[3] feels that lower-class youngsters begin school so poorly equipped to keep up with the academic demands that initial failure is almost inevitable, and the total school experience becomes negatively rather than positively reinforced. Many additional studies reveal that children who had unsatisfactory initial experiences in the school setting in their early years tend to continue to feel inadequate in the academic situation as long as they remain. These students are

---

[2]W. Brookover et al., Self-Concept of Ability and School Achievement, II, p. 251, Bureau of Educational Research Services, Michigan State, Univ., 1962.

[3]M. Deutsch, *The Disadvantaged Child*, pp. 18-20.

also more prone to drop out than are those who associate school with success and accomplishment from their first scholastic experiences.

In his study of Pennsylvania high school students, French[4] indicated the major reason for adolescents leaving school was simply because they did not like it.

Adolescents could be strongly and positively influenced by their school experiences were their teachers honest, unbiased, tolerant, inquisitive, and unafraid of intimacy. Young people frequently complain of feeling jailed at school with regulations, order, pressures, schedules, bells—everything but time to act independently and creatively. If teachers are not believed and respected their academic programs are doomed, and where can young people, alienated also from their parents, turn for guidance except to their peers?

There are few alternatives available to those who drop out of high school. A high school diploma is usually a minimal requirement for most jobs and often advanced training is required.

Parents who continue to support their adolescent who quits high school do him a great disservice. The sooner a young person sees the realities facing the dropout, the more likely he is to return to school or to begin preparation for a high school equivalency examination.

Although from the time they begin school youngsters are repeatedly impressed with the value of an education, they often feel that this is propaganda for the purpose of keeping them in school. (Incidentally, government studies suggest no correlation between grades and job success, but you will probably never hear school personnel admit this to be fact.) Many feel the education they are receiving is meaningless, and these same adolescents complain that their teachers are uninspired and report merely to collect their salaries. Some of their criticisms are valid, unfortunately. These complaints, however, do not justify dropping out.

---

[4]J. L. French, "Characteristics of High Ability Dropouts," pp. 67–69, *Bulletin of the National Association of Secondary School Principals*, 1969.

CASE HISTORY

When Roger's two best friends dropped out of school during their junior year of high school, he began to consider following suit. The only class he enjoyed was auto mechanics, and he felt certain that he could get a full-time job at his neighborhood filling station should he quit school. His friends encouraged him strongly to quit—one had a job as a busboy in a hotel restaurant and the other was still looking (albeit halfheartedly) for work after four weeks. They told Roger how great it was to be independent and to have some money of their own. The boy who was employed was entertaining all three—taking them out for beers and pool almost nightly. Luckily, Roger respected his parents and their feelings. He talked with them about his goals and how he knew he could presently make ends meet, despite his young years and lack of education, were he to drop out of school. They helped him to examine the long term situation and how much his position would improve several years hence were he to continue his education at least until he was awarded his high school diploma. Their remarks made an impression and he chose to remain in school while working part-time at a filling station.

It is definitely advantageous if early in life a child is taught the importance of staying with a task or project to its finish. It seems increasingly more common in this generation that a child enthusiastically begins something, quickly loses interest and drops it to turn to a new project. This is amply demonstrated by parents who let their youngster take piano lessons until he tires of them, move to tennis for a few sessions, switch to karate when tennis seems dull, and so forth. It is often these parents who wonder why their teenagers drop out of school when the going gets rough. It is the parents' responsibility to teach their youngsters to follow through.

Since salaries of young dropouts are usually small or nonexistent, many are forced to "bum" off their friends or to turn to delinquent or criminal dealings in order to survive. Small narcotics sales, thieveries, and "rip-offs" are common means of temporary support.

Enlightened dropouts who consider reenrollment in school often find that it is no easy matter. It would be beneficial if they were enthusiastically welcomed and encouraged by school administrators and faculty, but this too often is not the case. They instead find their reentry complicated by lectures and poor schedules coupled with unhopeful prognoses for success in completing their education. These young people need as much support as they can get from the adults in the scholastic setting, because commonly their peers will razz and humiliate them for their failure to "make it on the outside."

Many young people who remain in school strongly support the idea of their classmates dropping out. They may harbor secret dreams of doing this themselves, but prefer the vicarious experience through their friends' actions.

CASE HISTORY

Rachel quit school her senior year of high school. Her decision was based on her advanced pregnancy (five months) and her plans to marry. From the time she found that she was pregnant, she had been pleading that her boyfriend marry her and when that didn't work she resorted to threats. He tried to talk her into having an abortion or putting the child up for adoption, but she had hated school for the past few years and viewed her situation as the ideal excuse for dropping out. When he finally agreed to marriage, she was ecstatic and quit school that very day with only slightly less than a semester left to graduate. Her prospective husband, a dropout himself, placed little value on formal

education since he "was doing great as a tree-sprayer
—at least from spring through summer."

Often adolescents threaten to run away from home in an
effort to manipulate their parents. "If you don't let me stay
out until 1:00 A.M. like the rest of the kids, I'm moving out."
"I'll run away if you force me to go on a vacation with the
family." What is unfortunate both for parents and teenagers
is that tactics of this nature often work.

Many runaways "split" frequently—when things get tough
at home or at school, when they get bored or want attention
or when routine sets in. Some adolescents make halfhearted
attempts at running away. They frequently create a big scene
and pack (often making it clear where they can be reached
if the home situation is made more tolerable). Most of these
potential runaways are asking to be stopped. If they really
want to leave home there are more expedient and secretive
methods of doing it.

If these youngsters do go so far as to actually leave, they
usually return in a few days. They need little encouragement
to come home, but if they do happen to meet someone who
takes care of them, provides them with a place to stay, and
teaches them how to make it on the streets, their behavior is
reinforced.

An ideal time for a family meeting to air grievances and
to suggest alternatives is when running away is first mentioned by the young person to his parents.

Once a runaway has returned, either on his own or with
the "assistance" of law enforcement, he is usually given a
special status: preferred treatment at school, "Let's make it
more relevant for this disturbed youngster"; at home, "Where
have we gone wrong?"; at juvenile court, "What problems can
we help to alleviate?" This status, though short-lived, gives
temporary elevation to the runaway within his peer group.

Often youngsters run away from an intolerable problem
or from the fear of discovery of a situation in which they find
themselves, for example, a pregnancy, poor report card, or the

potential for being arrested on a drug or shoplifting charge. These adolescents see their leaving as the only alternative.

Others leave the home to escape from an abusive parent or parents. Certainly when many think of child abuse, they picture a battered child and a guilt-free, sadistic adult. This is anything but accurate. Child abuse can consist entirely of verbal abuse which can be at least as potentially damaging as physical abuse. The abusive parent is typically a depressed, passive-dependent, and alienated individual who was himself brought up by abusive parents. Neglect and abuse cut across all backgrounds and socioeconomic classes. Most frequently one child in the family is "picked out" for abuse; one who is perceived differently by his parents or one who really is different, i.e., brain damaged, gifted, or hyperactive. The abusive parent sees this youngster as bad, demanding, or perhaps stubborn. Usually some sort of crisis sets the abusive act into motion and most probably the youngster played no role in this crisis.

Abused children who are reared in this manner since infancy often bide their time until they find a way to split from the family scene. They typically have few guilt feelings about their desertion, feeling that their parents have amply demonstrated what they perceive as hatred toward them and subsequently they are desperately searching for love and acceptance. The abused runaway looks for a surrogate family or gang and usually will do almost anything for peer approval.

Sometimes well-intentioned parents harbor runaway friends of their youngsters in their homes. Many keep the child's whereabouts unknown while his parents frantically search for him, not even knowing whether he is safe. These parents should be advised that they risk facing charges of contributing to the delinquency of a minor by their actions. Frequently runaways paint such an intolerable picture of their home and parents that other adults feel sorry for them and try to assist. It is rarely helpful to those in either party for runaways to be welcomed at friends' homes. Adults should encourage these youngsters to return home and discuss their problems with their parents. They should not be put in the position of harborers or mediators and they should make their feelings clear.

Runaways are the first to admit that life on the street is no bed of roses and is full of many potential dangers, but it still offers a thrill and a feeling of independence that they feel makes up for the hunger, filth, and loneliness that many endure.

English terms the streetwise group, those who have been on the streets several years, as "hard road freaks." These are older teenagers who serve as role models for the young, naive runaway. "Much of their behavior resembles that of the traditional back street hustler. They engage in many street hustles such as dealing in drugs, pimping, prostitution, breaking and entering, and con jobs. In many cases they exploit their younger counterparts, the most common being male sexual exploitation of younger females."[5] While a very small number of runaways progress to becoming "hard road freaks," a sufficient amount of them do to insure the continuance of this phenomenon.

If at home and at school adolescents' emotional and achievement needs are met while they are still allowed the freedom to function within their particular group, they tend to experience the type of atmosphere from which no escape will be desired. In such an environment, young people grow to define their personal value systems and to act in accordance with them. This may involve chancing the consequences of peer rejection, but these adolescents are prepared to take such risks.

When confronted by the conflicting values of what they have been taught to believe vs. what they actually see practiced in our society, many young people in their hopelessness and alienation believe their only solution is to run—searching for a new life into which they feel they can be a part. Usually they return—to their homes and schools, but some do not.

---

[5]Clifford J. English, "Leaving Home: A Typology of Runaways." Copyright © 1973 by Transaction, Inc. Reprinted by permission of Transaction, Inc.

9 The Chemical Cop-Out: Drug Use and Abuse

Many young people who are extremely knowledgeable about the dangers of drug abuse will still partake because these risks are less threatening to them than are rejection and isolation. Some even pretend they use drugs to impress their peers. One youngster reported making dozens of needle marks in his arms so the kids would think he was shooting up, and when his parents saw these "track marks" they rushed him to the family physician. Only then did he admit that he was this desperate for acceptance.

Lynne, age fifteen: "It doesn't do that much for me, but at a party when they're passing a joint around, there's no way I can get out of smoking."

Melissa, age sixteen: "When the girls found out I wouldn't drink I was never invited to another slumber party. Now they call me a prude or just act as if I didn't exist."

CASE HISTORY

Robert, age seventeen: "If you'd told me even a year ago that I'd be a regular drug user—or even an experimenter—I'd have laughed you out of the room. I can't even believe it myself now. It was really such a gradual thing. In my early teens almost all of the kids in my group smoked dope, but that was about it. It finally became the reason for most gatherings—they didn't smoke and go to a dance—they got together to smoke, and to hell with the party. I really began to feel left out. They wouldn't ask me to do things with them often, but when they did, they'd tease me about being so straight and try to get me to try stuff. I guess I figured the reason I wasn't included was that they thought I was looking down on them because they were freaks. I decided to do it the next time I was asked. It wasn't any big thing—smoking pot, I mean. I don't think I even got stoned the first time or two. The kids seemed to like me a lot better when I smoked and I was among the first in the crowd to do acid and try other drugs. I'm really hooked on downers—but I'm finally accepted. It's a hell of a price."

CASE HISTORY

Shaun, age fifteen: "We were all invited to this guy's house and were asked to bring about a dozen of the prescription pills in our medicine cabinets at home. They mixed these all together in a big bowl and passed it around like popcorn. When I wouldn't take any they told me to get the hell out and then said if I told anybody, it would be the last thing I'd ever say."

In their study, Vener and his associates found that those who use drugs often begin early: "Five percent of the youngest students surveyed, those at age thirteen, reported some experience with drugs. The data supports those who seek to develop drug education, prevention, and therapy programs in the elementary schools."[1]

Often the "straights" are extremely suspect to the para-

[1]Arthur M. Vener, Cyrus S. Stewart, and David L. Hager, "Low Adolescent Use of Drugs," p. 385, School and Society, Dec. 1971.

noid drug group who frequently begin rumors that the non-users are working with narcotics agents to get them arrested. Many drug abusers and experimenters experience a pervasive fear that the "narcs" are tailing them and that they are subject to arrest at any time. They frequently go through rather elaborate precautions to avoid getting, in their terminology, "busted," and are constantly planning what to do and say if and when they are apprehended. This extreme suspicion is similar to that of the paranoid psychotic, though many fears of drug users are certainly based upon reality.

Taking drugs with a group is an experience which brings everybody closer together, many young people report. They say that nonusers "bring them down" so they can't have them around. Listening to a session of stoned young people reveals that much of their talk is in reference to: who is a "narc"; where they can make a connection; who can be trusted; who has to be "shut up"; whether they got "good stuff" or got "burned"; or how screwed-up society is.

Much is heard of the reported deep insights into self-awareness, finding of "truths," or enhancement of interpersonal rapport within the group; but to play back a tape recording of their so-called "meaningful experience" is an eye-opener to most. Most find their "meaningful experience" meaningless in the cold, hard light of day.

Many youngsters take drugs for one reason and one reason alone: group acceptance. Of course, there are those who use various drugs for other reasons, if all of their rationalizations may be taken at face value: to escape boredom; to get back at their parents (or the Establishment, authority figures, and so on); to "heighten" their sensitivity (or awareness, insight, reality); to fill a void in their lives; to have fun; to get through the school day; to get up for a party; to relax; to relieve anxiety. Several of these rationales should sound familiar to adults who use their favorite legalized drug, alcohol, for many of the same reasons.

A favorite story of drug educators is the one about the teenaged boy who took LSD rather regularly for "spiritual purposes." He came running into the room one day shouting,

"I've found it—I've found the secret of life!" His peers gathered around their leader, eager to hear the word. He proclaimed, *"The forces of the universe are flexible."* After much acclaim, one friend had the courage to ask what this meant, and the young man could not say. It must be said that some of the deep insights experienced while under the influence of even the milder hallucinogenic agents are less than profound, although many will take issue with this opinion.

Inhaling or "sniffing" volatile materials from spot removers or deodorants to hair sprays is popular among the very young adolescents. Glue and gasoline are the most popular substances and there are growing numbers of cases of accidents, erratic behaviors, and even deaths while under the influence of various sprays, glues, gasolines, and decongestants. Usually the older teenager, knowing of the potential danger of "sniffing," does not indulge, but for the youngster without funds to buy drugs, the highs he gets from everyday household sprays not only are available but also produce the desired effect at no expense.

One adolescent told his school counselor that he hoped that they would never legalize hallucinogenic drugs. She replied that she was in full agreement and was pleased to know that he had such a mature attitude. "Yes," he continued, "half the fun is sneaking around, outwitting the authorities, and getting away with it." This teenager is not unique in his feelings that playing cops and robbers is exciting and that much of the thrill is in the plotting, planning, hiding, and risking of their futures, together with proving how inadequate the law is in attempting to stop them. Sitting around talking about narrow escapes from the law is a favorite pastime for many in the drug culture.

Dealers usually have more status in the group than do the buyers, and having been through a few arrests grants to some even more peer approval. It often appears that the more vociferous or adamant parents become about not allowing their teenagers to associate with a certain group, the more enticing that crowd becomes to them. The forbidden fruit theory certainly applies in many of these instances.

Some of the criteria upon which parents' judgments are made regarding their children's friends certainly are poor indicators of drug involvement. The following are a few of the reasons parents refuse to let their teenagers associate with their friends: Length of hair, mode of dress, shifty eyes, beards, inability to talk with the parents, poor grades, dilated pupils of eyes, and dirtiness. It may come as a shock to some parents that many addicts have short hair, nice suits, straightforward looks, clean shaven faces and excellent scholastic records, and that they are extremely verbal and brighteyed and are even immaculately clean. Parental decisions should be based upon a more valid rationale, although it is understandable that many in this generation are turned off by some of the characteristics cited.

Some parents who have been suspecting for months that their children are using drugs are unable to substantiate their cases. They search their adolescents' cars, rooms, and pockets, listen in on their telephone calls, read notes and diaries, quiz their associates, and even spy on them. Some of these same parents might have saved themselves a great deal of worry and grief had they simply asked: "Are you using drugs?" A surprisingly large number of young people involved with drugs will respond honestly, perhaps because they are frightened and feel unable to cope with the situation alone. If parents can remain calm and supportive they may be able to work this through with their teenagers and outside intervention may not be necessary. In other situations professional help may be in order, particularly if the involvement has progressed beyond the experimental stage. Often family counseling has been particularly helpful in these cases, as is group counseling with peers experiencing similar difficulties.

Every parent is a role model for his child. The positive example he sets by minimizing *his* drug use will be a major step in preventing drug abuse by his children. Teenagers usually choose their own drugs rather than those of their parents for two reasons. First, it is their way of rebelling against the older generation—a perennial need for all adolescents. Secondly, by breaking away from their parents' customs, they establish their own identity, another of young people's long recognized needs.

Gross exaggerations of the effects of using marijuana by educators and parents alike have made this drug an excellent target for young people to demonstrate the hypocrisy of the Establishment. Certainly more study is necessary before the effects of long-term use of marijuana can be measured. There have been studies demonstrating cases of marijuana-induced temporary psychosis in the United States and many panic reactions have been reported, particularly among inexperienced users. In several Eastern countries this drug has been regarded as an important cause of psychosis. Research produces varying reports in this country, but clinical observations frequently indicate that regular use *may* contribute to the development of more passive, inward-turning, amotivational personality characteristics. For numerous adolescents the subtle change from conforming achievement-oriented behavior to a state of relaxed and careless drifting has been attributed to their use of significant amounts of marijuana.

Its use would also appear to increase the probable use of more dangerous drugs with higher potency, but many authorities would strongly disagree with this hypothesis. One of the largest studies of the association between marijuana and opiate addiction in the United States was compiled by Dr. John Ball, Chief of the Sociology Unit of the Addiction Research Center of the National Institute of Mental Health in 1968. He utilized a nationwide group of 2,213 addict patients, in whose cases the smoking of marijuana was seen as a predisposing influence in the etiology of opiate addiction. But as to the relative effect of marijuana use, as compared to delinquency or an unstable home, upon the development of opiate addiction—an adequate answer to this question is still not possible. Enough is known, however, about the association of marijuana and opiate use to determine a definite relationship between the use of the two drugs.

The potential opiate addict is predisposed to addiction by using marijuana for (*a*) both drugs produce a "high" (euphoric effect), (*b*) both drugs are available only through underworld sources, (c) both are used initially in a peer-group setting for recreation, and (d) both are illegal. Quite frequently both marijuana use and opiate use begin with the same group of friends, so one principal factor is that of primary association. In *Understanding Drug Use*, Marin and Cohen advise parents that if they are interested in helping the young develop criteria for defining an abuse of drugs, they might discuss some of the signs of excessive use of marijuana, hashish, or the psychedelics: "(1) increased problems in concentration, (2) failing memory, (3) increased paranoia and growing feelings of persecution, (4) growing underlying feelings of inferiority or exaggerated megalomania, (5) passivity and loss of energy, (6) difficulty with speech, increasing inability to get thoughts into words, (7) more difficulty with close relationships, (8) greater impulse toward destructiveness, (9) increasing feelings of futility and hopelessness, (10) the insistent denial to oneself that drugs might really be harmful."[2]

Even without drugs the abovementioned feelings may occur in the adolescent, but they do appear to accompany the excessive use of drugs.

According to Dr. Donald B. Louria, president of the New York State Council on Drug Addiction: "As the average age of those involved in drug abuse gets younger some of the new fads become progressively more bizarre. Young persons are smoking toothpaste and injecting peanut butter, milk, meat tenderizer, perfume, or mayonnaise by vein. Some people have even injected marijuana directly into the vein. As one might anticipate, the frequency of severe complications, death included, is very high."[3]

[2]Peter Marin, and Allan Y. Cohen, *Understanding Drug Use: An Adult's Guide to Drugs and the Young*, p. 59. Copyright © 1971 by Peter Marin and Allan Y. Cohen. Reprinted by permission of Harper & Row, Inc.

[3]Donald B. Louria, *Overcoming Drugs: A Program for Action.* Copyright © 1971 by Donald B. Louria. Used with permission of McGraw-Hill Book Company.

When considering the existing legal sanctions against the use of any drug, the questions to be considered include whether the laws actually deter or encourage use; how many would abuse the drug if legal control were removed; and if the drug abuser is a disturbed person who, if one drug is prohibited, will use another or some equally destructive behavior as a substitute. People are more vulnerable to the abuse of drugs in certain periods of life, including adolescence and other stressful periods. If a potential drug is unavailable at these times, it would appear that an undesirable chain of events could be avoided.

To the majority, regardless of the changing cultural attitudes and values, the freely chosen passive withdrawal to a life of drug-induced fantasy is an extremely threatening concept. Others argue that drug laws are attempts to legislate morality and that they evolved when the Protestant ethic and the competitive achievement-oriented value system prevailed. The adolescent of today, having never faced an economic depression, does not embrace the materialistic value system to the degree that his parents do. He also accepts pleasure in its own right rather than something needing to be earned as a reward for hard work. It does appear that laws will be moving in the direction of permitting greater individual freedom with respect to drug use.

Many parents are constantly vigilant in their search for adverse personality changes in their adolescents, not realizing that positive changes may also be attributed to drug use. A disinterested, apathetic young person may become much more alert and may bring home far better grades in the initial stages of amphetamine use; while a nervous, high strung child who flies off the handle at the slightest provocation may be much more manageable and agreeable while on barbiturates. Parents should know that rapid mood swings are a function of this age and are not usually related to the taking of drugs. But, when sudden changes in an adolescent for better or worse are dramatic and persistent, the causative agent *may* be drugs. Some frequently noted indicators include sudden changes in school attendance, reaction to discipline, academic performance, or unusual degrees of activity or inactivity, and irrational flare-ups involving strong emotion. Association with known drug abusers is quite frequently a sign of potential trouble.

No matter what has been stated by so-called experts, no one can effectively identify the majority of drugs by taste, sight, or smell, because most may be found in powder, capsule, tablet, and liquid forms and in a variety of colors or shapes. Only trained professionals through a series of laboratory procedures can correctly identify most drugs.

There is no way of determining whether educating young people about drugs has any effect whatsoever in diminishing drug usage. Accurate data about the incidence of drug experimentation and abuse are impossible to obtain. Most young people who take drugs are not about to talk about this with researchers and it is unlikely that they will be honest or cooperative when responding to surveys. A recent study within a public school system utilized a questionnaire where names were not to be used. The teachers were to leave the room while the youngsters filled out the forms. The students later made jokes about their responses; some pretending heroin habits, others writing that they had never been exposed to any drugs and one even confiding that he had accurate information that the school principal was "hooked" on tranquilizers. In almost all cases elaborate attempts to disguise their handwriting were devised, since the adolescents were certain the questionnaires would ultimately be handed over to the law.

The typical theme in drug education programs is the "scare the hell out of them" approach. The show opens with a former addict endlessly listing his horrible decline into the pit of human depravity. This is followed by a local physician exaggerating bodily harm brought about by drugs, climaxed with perhaps a few slides of deformed babies produced by addicts. The program ends with a law enforcement agent who will tell of the excellent young people he has personally

Identification of Drug Abusers*†

General Symptoms

- Abrupt changes in school or work attendance, quality of work, grades, discipline, work output
- Unusual flare-ups or outbreaks of temper
- Withdrawal from responsibility
- General changes in overall attitude
- Deterioration of physical appearance and grooming
- Furtive behavior regarding actions and possessions
- Wearing of sunglasses at inappropriate times (to hide dilated or constricted pupils)
- Continual wearing of long-sleeved garments (to hide injection marks)
- Association with known drug abusers
- Unusual borrowing of money from parents or friends
- Stealing small items from home, school, or employer
- Attempts to appear inconspicuous in manner and appearance (to avoid attention and suspicion)
- May frequent odd places without cause, such as storage rooms, closets, basements (to take drugs)

The Glue Sniffer (or User of Other Vapor-Producing Solvents)

- Odor of substance on breath and clothes
- Excess nasal secretions, watering of eyes
- Poor muscular control
- Drowsiness or unconsciousness
- Increased preference for being with a group, rather than being alone
- Plastic or paper bags or rags, containing dry plastic cement or other solvent, found at home or in locker at school or at work

The Depressant Abuser (barbiturates, tranquilizers, "downs")

- Symptoms of alcohol intoxication with one important exception: no odor of alcohol on breath
- Staggering or stumbling
- Falling asleep inexplainably
- Drowsiness; may appear disoriented
- Lack of interest in school and family activities

The Stimulant Abuser (amphetamines, cocaine, "speed," "bennies," "ups")

- Pupils may be dilated (when large amounts have been taken)
- Mouth and nose dry; bad breath; user licks his lips frequently
- Goes long periods without eating or sleeping
- Excessive activity; user is irritable, argumentative, nervous; has difficulty sitting still
- Chain smoking
- If injecting drug, user may have hidden eye droppers and needles among possessions

The Narcotic Abuser (heroin, morphine)

- Lethargic, drowsy
- Inhaling heroin in powder form leaves traces of white powder around nostrils, causing redness and rawness
- Pupils are constricted and fail to respond to light
- Injecting heroin leaves scars, usually on the inner surface of the arms and elbows, although user may inject drugs in body where needle marks will not be seen as readily
- Users often leave syringes, bent spoons, bottle caps, eye droppers, cotton and needles in lockers at school or hidden at home

The Marijuana Abuser

- In the early stages of intoxication, may appear animated with rapid, loud talking and bursts of laughter
- In the later stages, may be sleepy or stuporous
- Pupils usually are dilated
- Odor (similar to burnt rope) on clothing or breath
- Remnants of marijuana, either loose or in partially smoked "joints" in clothing or possessions
- Usually user in a group, at least in early habit of smoking

Note: Unless under the influence of the drug at the time of observation, marijuana users are difficult to recognize; infrequent users may not show any of the general symptoms of drug abusers. Marijuana is greener than tobacco. Cigarettes made of it (called "joints," "sticks" or "reefers") are rolled in a double thickness of brown or off-white cigarette paper. Smaller than a regular cigarette, with the paper twisted or tucked in at both ends, the butts (called "roaches") are not discarded but saved for later smoking if not consumed at initial usage. Marijuana also may be smoked in a pipe (very small bowl, long stem) or cooked in brownies and cookies.

The LSD (or STP, DMT, THC) Abuser

- Users usually sit or recline quietly in a dream or trancelike state
- Users may become fearful and experience a degree of terror which makes them attempt to escape from the group
- Senses of sight, hearing, touch, body-image, and time are distorted
- Mood and behavior are affected, the manner depending upon emotional and environmental condition of the user
- Users may have unpredictable flashback episodes without use of the drug

Note: It is unlikely that persons using LSD or other hallucinogens will do so in school, at work, or at home at a time when they might be observed. At least in the early stages of usage, these drugs generally are taken in a group situation under special conditions designed to enhance their effect.

LSD is odorless, tasteless, and colorless. It may be injected, but usually is taken orally in impregnated sugar cubes, cookies, or crackers.

---

*This outline may help you identify persons abusing drugs by enabling you to recognize symptoms and signs of drug abuse. Obviously, no one symptom should be considered an indication of such abuse. Also, it should be remembered that some of these symptoms could indicate normal adolescent variability or other health problems. In other words, SYMPTOMS ARE NOT PROOF. CONCLUSIONS SHOULD BE BASED ON FACT, NOT ASSUMPTIONS.

†Reprinted from *Teaching about Drugs: A Curriculum Guide, K-12* with permission of the American School Health Association and the Pharmaceutical Manufacturers Association.

Guide to Drugs: Effects, Uses, and Regulation

NAME OF DRUG	USUAL SHORT-TERM EFFECTS	LEGITIMATE ACTUAL AND POSSIBLE MEDICAL USES
STIMULANTS Amphetamines	Central Nervous System (C.N.S.) stimulants. Increased alertness, reduction of fatigue, loss of appetite, insomnia or paranoia, euphoria.	Treatment of obesity, narcolepsy, fatigue, depression.
Cocaine	Same.	Anesthesia of the eye and throat.
BARBITURATES Nembutal Seconal Phenobarbital	C.N.S. depressants. Sleep induction. Relaxation (sedation). Sometimes euphoria. Drowsiness. Impaired judgment, reaction time, coordination, and emotional control. Relief of anxiety tension. Muscle relaxation.	Treatment of insomnia and tension. Induction of anesthesia.
ALCOHOL	C.N.S. depressant. Relaxation (sedation). Sometimes euphoria. Drowsiness. Impaired judgment, reaction time, coordination, and emotional control. Frequent aggressive behavior, driving accidents.	Rare. Sometimes as a sedative for tension.
TRANQUILIZERS Librium Thorazine Compazine Stelazine Reserpine	Selective C.N.S. depressants. Relaxation, relief of anxiety tension. Suppression of hallucinations or delusions; improved functioning.	Treatment of anxiety, tension, alcoholism, neurosis, psychosis, psychosomatic disorders, and vomiting.
NARCOTICS Opium Heroin Morphine Codeine	C.N.S. depressants. Sedation, euphoria, relief of pain, impaired intellectual functioning and coordination.	Treatment of severe pain, diarrhea, cough.
VOLATILE CHEMICALS Glue Gasoline	When used for mind-altering effects, generally produce a "high" (euphoria) with impaired coordination and judgment.	None.
PSYCHEDELICS LSD Mescaline Psilocybin THC in cannabis (marijuana, hashish)	Production of visual imagery, increased sensory stimulation, anxiety, nausea, impaired coordination; sometimes consciousness alteration. Occasional psychotic episodes. In lower doses, relaxation, euphoria, slight depression, occasional increase in appetite, alteration in time sense and lesser impairment of judgment and coordination.	Experimental study of the mind and brain functions. Treatment of alcoholism, mental illness in controlled psychotherapeutic settings. In lower doses, treatment of depression, loss of appetite, and minor neuroses.

POTENTIAL FOR PHYSICAL DEPENDENCE	POTENTIAL FOR PSYCHOLOGICAL DEPENDENCE	FORM OF LEGAL REGULATION AND CONTROL
Debatable (depending on doses)	High	Amphetamines—same as barbiturates below.
Same		Cocaine—same as narcotics below.
Yes	High	Available by ordinary medical prescription. Widely advertised and "detailed" to MDs and pharmacists. Other manufacture, sale, or possession prohibited under federal drug abuse laws and similar state drug laws. Moderate penalties. Widespread illicit traffic.
Yes	High	Available and advertised in many forms without limitation. Only minimal regulation. Minimal penalties.
No	Moderate	Same as barbiturates above. Not usually included under the special federal or state drug laws.
Yes	High	Available (except heroin) by special (narcotics) medical prescriptions. Some available by ordinary prescription or over the counter (e.g., codeine). Other manufacture, sale, or possession prohibited under state and federal narcotics laws. Severe penalties. Extensive illicit traffic.
No	Minimal to Moderate	Generally easily available. In several states, sale of glue is banned to those under 21.
Tentatively no	Minimal to High (depending on individual)	**Strong psychedelics:** available only to a few medical researchers (or to members of the Native American Church). Other manufacture, sale, or possession prohibited by state dangerous drug laws or federal drug abuse laws. Moderate penalties. Extensive illicit traffic. **Marijuana and hashish:** unavailable (although permissible) for ordinary medical prescription. Possession, sale, and cultivation prohibited by state and federal narcotic or marijuana laws. Severe penalties. Widespread illicit traffic.

known who have been ruined or have died as a result of drug abuse. This approach does not work for one simple reason—*the kids know better!* Many have already been there or, at least, part way there. They do know that if the effects of a "soft" drug they have already experienced are hideously exaggerated, chances are good that the effects of others have been as well. As educators become more sophisticated they are beginning to add participants to their program who provide more factual knowledge about drugs.

Parents should thoroughly acquaint themselves with the drug laws at the local, state, and federal levels and make certain their children know these penalties as well. Also they must let them know the future consequences of what may seem to the young as very harmless acts, for example, no vote, incarceration, no military service, no admission to law schools or other professional programs.

One drug noticeably conspicuous by its absence in the majority of education programs is alcohol—and adolescents are quick to point out that our "socially approved" drug is America's number one health problem. Many adults are often too busy attacking adolescents' preferred drugs and too hypocritical to mention alcohol, which is becoming increasingly popular with young people as well.

A recent Triangle Research Institute study involving over thirteen thousand students from thirteen to eighteen years of age in 450 schools across the country revealed about twenty-eight percent of the nation's students are problem drinkers. This study also found that about one of every four thirteen-year-olds in the nation, or twenty-four percent, can be considered "moderate" drinkers. Over half of the students reported that they had been drunk within the past year and the ranks of teetotaling teenagers dwindled steadily with age, from the high of thirty-eight percent at age thirteen to less than half that by age seventeen.

According to Brickman, "The intense drive to divest oneself from dependence upon parents and other elders has given way to conformity with the chronological age group. The highest values seem to be the satisfaction of curiosity and the yearning for 'kicks.' "[4] He feels that what might help to solve the problem would be an exertion and extension of effort by the family, as well as by social, educational, and religious groups, to provide a positive inspiration to youth in order to reduce their need to depend upon drugs.

Drug slang constantly changes, as Richard R. Lingeman notes. His book about drugs is in dictionary form, and is an excellent reference source for parents and educators. In his preface, he voices what so many parents have said in various ways: "When I was in college, drugs were things you bought at the drugstore. Oh, there was a small Benzedrine scene on campus around exam time, and one read about marijuana in Jack Kerouac, who was then in vogue, but an offer of marijuana probably would have been turned down without the slightest compunction. In those benighted days, in the early fifties, our "up," if we indeed had one, was Ortlieb's beer. LSD had been discovered but, if someone had mentioned it, we would probably have thought he meant an honorary degree."[5]

Researchers studying committed drug users often feel that the reasons for continuing to take a drug are frequently different from the reasons for starting it. To use cigarettes as an example, one may start to smoke because the other kids are doing it and it makes him feel grown up, but the smoking persists because he *needs* that cigarette: to stay content, to suppress tension, or for any of a number of other reported reasons; certainly including a desire to stave off withdrawal symptoms.

There are many fine young people who use drugs only when they are going to be with others, because without drugs they feel tense, anxious, and nervous. A phenomenon gener-

---

[4]William W. Brickman, "Drug Addiction and the Schools," p. 147, *School and Society,* Feb. 1971.

[5]Richard R. Lingeman, *Drugs from A to Z: A Dictionary.* Copyright © 1969 by Richard R. Lingeman. Used with permission of McGraw-Hill Book Company.

ally noted in drug users is their inability to function well socially with the opposite sex. By using these agents, many of the anxieties which are difficult to resolve in the process of growing up can be alleviated or even forgotten.

Drugs can remove their users from intimacy although their feelings about drugs are that they do the exact opposite. While under the influence of drugs young people often discuss their caring and love, not only for each other, but for all humanity. Ironically, when they come off the drugs they tend to sneak back into their corners where they do not have to look at each other again.

Steffenhagen[6] notes that some students quit using drugs when they become socially involved, explaining that they have not had time to do drugs lately. In these cases, the drug use is not pathological; it is merely a social outlet.

Another relevant factor in adolescents' use of drugs is probably disillusionment; the sad response of facing the harsh life and reality of an unkind society that comes one day to most young people. If a way out through drugs is available, it may become very attractive indeed. Young people often believe that they are invulnerable and this also contributes to their problem—that *they* can't get hooked or get in over their heads. Their peers appear to handle drugs well, so they know they can, too. Curiosity cannot be dismissed as it is an important contributory factor in many initial drug-experimenting situations.

Although we cannot feel that many of these reasons for trying drugs are good ones, the point is not whether we like them, whether they are real or unreal, good or bad. The point is that young people do believe, or profess to believe these reasons, so adults must try to understand them.

To change their lives, since to live them "straight" would be intolerable, more and more youngsters are altering their states of consciousness and perception. McAcree and his col-

---

[6]Ronald A. Steffenhagen, "Drug Abuse and Related Phenomena: An Adlerian Approach," p. 243, *Journal of Individual Psychology,* Nov. 1974.

leagues[7] found that it is the potentially more disturbed individual who seems to be attracted toward the potentially more dangerous forms of drugs.

If exciting alternatives were offered to the young, the abuse of drugs would probably decline. Unfortunately, some of the proposed activities are more threatening to adults than are drugs. These include various kinds of psychotherapy, encounter and sensitivity groups, awareness exercises, spiritual disciplines, Yoga, Zen, silence, meditation, experiences in the wilderness, political involvement, experimental and "free" schools and universities, youth communes, arts, crafts, drama, and music. Many of these alternatives seem strange to parents for whom the pep club, football team, or Junior Red Cross were acceptable outlets which were satisfying and rewarding in their day. Young people's needs and interests have changed tremendously and they feel an almost universal desire to reach out and to widen their experiences in different directions.

By the community's making the abovementioned options available, however self-consciously, adults will not have a written guarantee that the young will choose them instead of drugs. Activities of this nature *may* make adolescents' lives more tolerable or meaningful, and *could* alleviate part of the drug problem. Certainly the methods presently being used to combat drug experimentation and abuse are less than effective, if one relies on either current statistics or adolescents' reports.

---

[7]C. P. McAcree et al., *Personality Factors in College Drug Users*, p. 105.

10 Radicals, Rebellion, and Street People

For many young people in large cities, street life begins early. Youngsters have to prove their "manliness," toughness, and daring from their elementary school years on, and often shared illegal activities are the bonds that tie them together in a sense of family or solidarity. Trust or loyalty has always been an important variable but the element of competition within the gang and the importance of group ranking are usually of prime significance.

Fighting is often the principal instrument of ranking, particularly in the gangs of younger adolescents. The older teenage gangs traditionally judge their members on what they term courage, but some even rate on what drugs they use—the stronger the drug, the more status in the group. To be included they must take risks and must show a disregard for the law, but must particularly prove to their crowd that they are in charge, that no one else (particularly a parent) is "calling the shots." They must be *big men*, flaunting the rules and regulations followed by others, and by so doing prove to their peers that they are worthy of membership; that they are answerable to no one but their members and are indomitable. Only then may they be considered for inclusion by the gang.

Henry Miller and Jim Baumohl report in "*Down and Out in Berkeley*" that "poverty is the hallmark of the street person. Whereas the hippie was the child of the affluent middle class, the street person is the child of the working class."[1]

The hippies, whose movement peaked in the late sixties, dropped out of adult society to demonstrate their disgust for materialism, hypocrisy, and power, and their opposition to violence and wars. Hippies assumed unorthodox dress and many gave up their educations and jobs to live in poverty and to share whatever they had with their peers. Many had trouble with the law due in part to their use of marijuana and psychedelic drugs, to their behavior at youth festivals, and to the fact that they were often runaways. Of course a large percentage of the young and even middle aged adopted hippie dress and hairstyles but did not pursue their lifestyle. Certainly the hippies set the example for those involved in the rebellious movements currently prevalent.

The street people of today bear only a superficial resemblance to the flower children of the sixties. They do not seem to be anti-establishment due to their ideology. The majority of street people are male, white, under twenty-five years of age and high school dropouts. They are authentically poor and unemployed because they lack the education, training, references, or apparel that are necessary for seeking employment in today's job market. They are quite vocal about employers' discrimination against them, due particularly to their appearance. Many street people say that this is typical of the misplaced values of modern society—that we judge by who people know and what they look like rather than the important attributes they possess. They then can rationalize that society has the problem, not they; and who wants to be a part of a society so hypocritical?

Many youngsters on the street today are alcoholics; some are as young as fifteen or sixteen years of age. They can be compared to the skid row bums of yesterday, except the latter dropped out late in life, not early. Statistics show that approximately 1.3 million boys and girls between the ages of

---

[1]Quoted in Patricia Horn et al., "Street People—A Growing Urban Problem" p. 20, *Psychology Today,* May 1975.

twelve and seventeen have serious drinking problems and that alcohol-related arrests of youngsters have increased seven hundred percent over the past five years. To feel removed, anesthetized, and numb most must steal or prostitute themselves to support their habits.

CASE HISTORY

"I can't remember when I had my first drink. I couldn't have been out of grade school, though. I know that by seventh grade I was snitching alcohol from my parents' and my friends' houses. I especially needed it before an 'occasion'—a date, a big test...whatever. It finally got so I would manufacture 'occasions.' I got caught several times in ninth grade and my sophomore year. I drank before school every morning so I could face my fellow prisoners and our wardens. Dad threatened to kick me out of the house if I didn't lay off. He couldn't understand that I was way past that point— I couldn't stop. I split that year and I've been on the streets for almost a year now. I don't think my folks have tried to find me and I don't blame them. A fifteen-year-old alcoholic in the family would be rather awkward to explain to their friends. I thought when all the pressure was off I could handle booze, but it's worse than it ever was."

Many street people privately admit that they want to rejoin society but cannot, because by so doing they would in effect be backing down. Often they state that if they could return to the mainstream of traditional life without their families and friends saying "I told you so" or "You finally came to your senses," they would do so, but they say they cannot bear to face statements of this nature, so they continue their unorthodox lifestyles. Joseph Katz[2] says: "There

[2]Joseph Katz, "Rearing Rads, Rebs, and Regulars," pp. 9–10, *PTA Magazine,* Aug. 1970.

are many different ways of expressing dissent. Studies have shown that there are differences between young people who are alienated from society but actively work toward its reform and those who retreat individually or in groups to a special world of their own. The former may be called radicals—though activists is becoming the more common term—the latter, rebels. One study suggests that each of these different attitudes has one of its roots in the family situation. The combination of a domineering mother and a weak, ineffectual father tends to produce, particularly in sons, rebellious withdrawal. The activist is more likely to have a father whom he respects and who is assertive."

Researchers indicate that student activists are neither the troublemakers nor those on academic probation one might suspect would be the case, but on the contrary, they have achieved academically to a greater degree than have their classmates. Their parents generally are professionals of a high income group who reared their children according to the methods suggested by the current child psychology experts. The typical activist has been found to be up on current events, imaginative, creative, and willing to take risks to work for the improvement of society. Many have rejected materialistic goals and have attained fulfillment by working in the Peace Corps, consumer reform, penal institutions, civil rights, political organizations, or for the underprivileged; often they work for minimum wages or merely for room and board. Their idealism often becomes tarnished after a few months or years of working for their particular cause and most then return to the nine-to-five white-collar world of their parents. The disillusionment they speak of is disheartening, but those who wish to marry and have children realize that the money necessary for this precludes their contributing to societal reform as a full-term career.

" 'It isn't birth control we need, it's control of what we've already given birth to.' The speaker was a father—one who had gone along with 'authorities' who said that children should be free to express themselves and who now saw in student riots the frightening result of a generation of over-permissiveness.' "[3]

Since the typical modern parent has turned from the strict discipline of his grandparents, if not his own parents, he is beginning to wonder if he has not gone overboard, providing his young with everything so that they feel no need to do anything or to become somebody. Some parents are too afraid of their own children to give them real guidance so they alternate between permissiveness and punitiveness, finding no solution in their inconsistency. They clear all obstacles before their children, leaving none for them to overcome.

Overpermissiveness cannot be blamed for all of society's ills, but there is no question that it has played a primary role. Parents' fear of denying their children's every whim has left the young with little frustration tolerance. When things do not go their way as they approach adulthood, many decide to get even by striking back or by dropping out.

Research indicates that occasionally college or high school students will admit that they participate in protests, marches, and anti-establishment demonstrations only for the shock effect; principally to embarrass their parents or to show them that they find their generation's complacency and value system irrelevant and lacking. Many of these youngsters who in effect are thumbing their noses at everything their parents stand for are also standing with their hands out for money for tuitions, cars, and allowances—although they profess to deplore the materialistic world of the older generation.

However angry young people are about social injustice, the majority express a philosophical rather than an overt rebelliousness. Primarily they express an intention to work within the system to effect desirable changes.

The FBI's Uniform Crime Reports show forty-four percent of the nation's murderers are twenty-five or younger and ten percent are under eighteen. Seventy-five percent of all

---

[3]Augusta Graham, "A Parent's Manifesto—Our Grievances," p. 3, *PTA Magazine,* March 1970.

crimes, excluding murder, were committed by persons under twenty-five and forty-five percent by persons under eighteen. Police officials attribute much of the juvenile crime to street gangs. Recent reports indicate that almost three hundred gangs exist in New York City alone with an estimated membership of 18,500.

Anthropologist Walter Miller, Harvard University Institute of Criminal Justice, believes there has been a drastic change in youngsters. He feels many are becoming inhuman and amoral people: "Gangs are really more violent today. There's more validity to that statement than at any time in the past."[4]

Some sociologists attribute this phenomenon to the violence today's young person grew up with watching murders, rapes, and other sadistic behaviors on television. Others point to the breakdown of the family unit or the disrespect young people demonstrate toward authority figures, the government, their parents, and law enforcement. Most research indicates that family background and community size have little impact on the rate of juvenile delinquency.

Researchers at the Institute for Juvenile Research in Chicago note that a pattern of general disregard for the law exists among today's young people. Young activists speak of the realities of the inequities of our system of jurisprudence, of police brutality, and of governmental intelligence agencies' infiltration that has occurred on several campuses.

Inadequate personality types (compliant, dependent, and conforming) mirror the personalities of people they are with; they take on their causes and their ideologies for acceptance. These are the people for whom recruits for radical movements are looking. These are the young people, lacking in strong senses of personal identities and self-esteems, who will readily comply with their leaders if only they are made to feel a part of a "family" or "gang." They will engage in

---

[4]Quoted in "Street Gangs Intensify Violence Toward Public," *Tulsa Daily World,* Nov. 4, 1975, p. A17.

illegal activities, reject their early teachings and even their families if they can convince themselves that their rebellion will give them a sense of personal worth and peer acceptance. The term brainwashing apparently was coined by Edward Hunter, an American journalist, as a translation of a Chinese colloquialism, *hsi nao* (wash brain). This word was first used during the Communist Chinese takeover to describe their indoctrination techniques. Brainwashing emerged again during the trial of Patricia Hearst; her defense counsel's leaning heavily on the heretofore untested legal theory that the Symbionese Liberation Army brainwashed their captor.

Apparently brainwashing can be accomplished by several methods, but it usually begins with an attack on one's sense of identity; instilling feelings of guilt, disorientation, and virtual self-annihilation. Usually then the victim is reindoctrinated, or "reborn"; instilled with his "captors' " ideologies. Researchers in this area stress that an isolated environment is essential in this process and that victims must receive no communication from the outside world.

Sociologist Kirt Lang, who has studied both dramatic shifts in philosophy and religious conversion, feels that people of strong convictions, if they have no hidden insecurities, are least susceptible to brainwashing. Often monogamous sexual relations within revolutionary groups are abandoned with all sexual needs met by comrades within the group. To maintain harmony and overcome jealousies, exclusive relationships are taboo.

Some studies of American POWs who had been "brainwashed" indicated that only fifteen percent were successfully converted; this leads one to believe that a basic morality system, once established, is tenacious. Certainly many so-called conversions are temporary.

To bring about a radically reorganized belief system, a person must be separated from anyone who shares his beliefs, who can be supportive. This individual must be forced to examine and question his loyalties and moral stance.

Physical pressures (deprivation of food and sleep) are often utilized, and cooperative victims are rewarded. To give up or renounce one's past is continually hammered into the "captive's" head.

Usually absolute obedience is demanded.

It appears that a young person with no great sense of self or belongingness can easily be caught up in the excitement of a radical organization, feeling he can prove to his group that he is worthy of membership, that he can help to accomplish their goals, ranging from saving America from itself by revolution to attacking a specific organization or agency.

The close correlation between the alleged brainwashing in the Hearst case, admittedly more savage, and the militaristic indoctrination in isolated centers of some of the new religious cults certainly bears noting, and some social scientists have paralleled brainwashing with religious conversions (see page 120).

Many young people feel they are being trained by their parents and teachers to become automatons, adding more victims to the indistinguishable members of the silent majority. This they will fight; holding responsible the schools, the church, the news media, and/or the capitalist society into which they perceive themselves as being molded. They believe in change by any means necessary and see themselves as psychological victims of society's sickness.

Most radical high school youngsters are less concerned about fighting vague concepts such as "imperialism" and are more involved with issues such as dress codes and smoking regulations. Subversive groups exploit issues as minor as these to get across to the student that the Establishment is attempting to turn him into a robot with no rights and to convince him to focus on the administrator, usually the principal, to see him as a dictator. The group may then try to manipulate the other students, parents, and teachers to harass the administration and may even attempt to gain community support by publishing underground newspapers, holding workshops, and encouraging students to participate in demonstrations.

The adolescent who is popular with his peer group and who wants to stay in the social swing is particularly susceptible to temptation if his group involves itself in borderline-delinquent behavior. Since he is so involved with his peers, their opinions subtly become part of his own motivational and behavioral set. Those who have already been judged unacceptable by their peers are less likely to identify with these attitudes. If the "in-crowd" is drinking, smoking pot, or stealing C.B.s, so is the youngster struggling to maintain his position with his group. If he refuses such involvement, he is branded immature or cowardly and is ostracized until he goes along with his peers.

CASE HISTORY

Chris, age fifteen, was the leader of his gang. He introduced them to liquor (stolen from his parents' bar) to pills (again, from his family's medicine cabinet) and was the first of his peers to "go all the way" with a girl. He was the only one in his crowd with a car (his parents bought it for him, although he was underaged and not licensed) and generally led the way in deviant and illegal behavior in his crowd. When his friend Conrad suggested "ripping off" stereo-tape decks from cars in shopping centers, Chris vetoed the idea. Conrad suggested Chris was "chicken" and the group agreed. They polled their members, elected Conrad as their new chief, and gave Chris the option of either getting out or following the orders of his new leader. Chris followed.

Most parents hope that their children will not reject or retreat from society or attempt to overthrow it, but instead will devote their energies and intelligence into reforming it. When adults honestly confront themselves with their own lives, they may be able to begin to understand that those who have dropped out of our society or have attempted to overthrow or to reform it have done so rather than to imitate their elders. Few adults find their lives tolerable, much less joyful; many, in fact, live in a detached numb avoidance of reality.

Young people know this and they do not want it for themselves. So they set themselves adrift, knowing that they will be giving up creature comforts, but knowing, too, that for them this is far preferable to submission to the traditional lifestyles of their elders. Or the extremists rise up against contemporary society and prepare to give up their lives rather than to conform.

If parents could cut their pretense and posture that they have found the answers and now want to impart them to their children to help them see the light, there would probably be less overt rebellion or escapism. Our honesty about our own doubts, anguish, and even despair at times, coupled with our real and active commitment to societal betterment, can set an example our youth can not only relate to but can also join. Our respect and emotional support may facilitate this process.

11 Cultism, Off-Beat Religious Practices, and Witchcraft

"Man, recognizing his own mortality, and hoping deep down to find a cure for the condition, has always grasped for straws. This understandable longing for immortality has led to many complex and fascinating beliefs."[1]

Magic, occult, witchcraft, demons, ghosts, supernatural, astral projection, unidentified flying objects, extrasensory perception, astrology, psychic powers—the unknown is universally intriguing and has been in all ages.

Numerous religious cults have mushroomed in the last few years. Young people by the thousands have joined the Jesus People, Children of God, Hare Krishna, the Unification Church of Sun Myung Moon, and countless other gurus and mystics.

A close examination reveals a similar thread running throughout many of these movements. There is frequently a successful leader who has tightly organized his followers with an astute eye toward fund raising. Members must be totally dedicated and willing to make personal sacrifices for the Cause.

The individual who joins these minority groups often desires freedom from responsibility; he can lean on somebody to make his decisions and gain almost instant acceptance by a group of similar "followers," thereby enhancing his self-esteem.

---

[1]Bernhardt J. Hurwood, *Passport to the Supernatural,* p. 14.

Unfortunately, many of our traditional churches seem formal, punitive, and irrelevant to our young. The services and programs have not changed substantially to meet their needs and they often discontinue attendance when their parents permit it; a time which frequently coincides with early adolescence. Many prefer to explore and question the religious tenets they may have blindly accepted as children, but they are made to feel oppressed and isolated when they challenge established dogmas.

Many of our youth find the search for religious consciousness and human potential stimulating. At Esalen, California, a well-known growth center, an intellectual judgment has been set forth—"You don't have to be sick to get better." Young religious zealots attempt to look beneath the superficial aspects of spiritual convictions to discover basic truths and to change their lives accordingly. They then may feel an obligation to help their peers discover a similar enlightenment and destiny.

Certainly only a very small percentage of American youngsters have joined mystical, prophetic, occult, or oriental religious sects, but the question still remains: Why?

Sociologists studying these cults have determined that for the most part participants have been dissatisfied, average middle-class teenagers who expected more from life than they were given—particularly a sense of significance, belongingness, or personal worth. They have not been youngsters who were reared in an overly zealous religious environment nor were they from homes lacking in religious instruction. Most of the young Americans involved in the so-called "guru" cults were reared in traditional Christian and Jewish faiths. They cannot be equated with the young people who join radical political groups: activists, militants, or terrorists—those wanting to overthrow existing societal institutions. They do, however, express a deep dissatisfaction for typical middle-class morality as they perceive it, and see as empty or meaningless the goals and ideals of their elders: a three bedroom home with no mortgage, two cars, a two-week vacation with pay, and college educations for their kids. They also perceive the Establishment as hypocritical, the "do as I say and not as I do" approach being cited by many: "Sure my folks went to church every Sunday and saw to it that I never missed Sunday school either. The most important part was what we should wear—or maybe even more important was that we be seen: the typical happy 'those who pray together, stay together' American family. It didn't matter that everybody probably knew that Dad was making it with his secretary, that Mom had a drinking problem or that my brother and I hit up. All that was forgotten as we piously kneeled together in prayer, setting an example to the community as a loving, God-fearing, and successful family."

Those in the Jesus movement, for the most part, do not seem to be bright, deep-thinking, introspective, or philosophically bent youngsters; they are loners who want to *belong*; to have a sense of family unitedness and direction. They passively and often without question accept the precepts and dictates of their "leader." They look to him for the answers and often for the strong father figure so lacking in their pasts. Each movement's central figure appears strong and evidences considerable personal charisma. Followers become expert in parroting the leader's teachings after hours of memorization of his edicts, so they frequently appear extremely knowledgeable and wise.

So many "off-beat" religious cults stress heightening their converts' subjective consciousness and attempting to destroy their objective awareness of reality. This totally absolves their cult from social responsibility and is appealing to the tuned-out young. It is as if the only important goal should be "getting one's head together"; they forget that there is a world outside beset with problems and responsibilities that one must face to effect reform and change. An egocentric, confused youngster who does not want to face the trials, tribulations, and guilts he saw the previous generation endure finds this escape inviting.

Self-proclaimed prophets are exploiting and victimizing thousands of anxious young people discouraged by our unsettled times and their overly permissive upbringings. Many

desire commitment to a strong cause involving deep emotional-
ism and reform—a need apparently met more by cult and
occult groups than by traditional religions.

Parental accusations that youngsters are "brainwashed"
into soliciting money while sacrificing intellectual freedom are
becoming frequent. Rabbi Maurice Davis, who heads Citizens
Engaged In Reuniting Families, an organization of parents
and excultists, believes that the young people are brainwashed. "The more I get into it, the more frightened I become," he says. "The constant hammering on a single theme
at training centers, the use of fatigue, the intensity of the
programs—all these things combine to break young people.
Afterward, you look in their eyes and know. that something
is wrong."[2]

Certainly those heading the cults deny all charges, pro-
claiming that all truly committeed to a cause may seem
changed, but that brainwashing and coercion tactics are not
employed. A recent phenomenon is the profession of "depro-
grammers." These are people, usually hired by parents, who
help persuade youngsters out of the new mystical and religious groups.

When January 1974 had come and gone, the followers
of the Children of God sect began to dissipate, at least in the
United States. That was the month "Moses" David Berg, se-
cluded founder of the group, had predicted that the Comet Ko-
houtek would explode, destroying America. When this act of
God didn't come off, "Moses" became even more of a recluse.

The Children's ranks seem to be diminishing, not only
because of "Moses' " false prophecy, but probably also because
the letters he mails to his converts have become more and
more sexually oriented; even pornographic. The C.O.G. information center is now in London, and "Moses" still mails
his weekly epistles, called "Mo Letters" to his converts. Moses
is preaching a line unusual to the Jesus Movement:
sexual freedom.

---

[2]George W. Cornell, "Those 'Guru' Cults—Religion or Exploitation?"
p. 100, *Reader's Digest*, Feb. 1976.

"Thanks, and you have a good day, too"

Leo I. Caravan

One thing may be said for this movement, however; the Children are still tremendously efficient in their indoctrination of converts, even in the face of the prophecies of their leader not coming to pass.

In the early seventies when the C.O.G. first appeared, parents throughout the country accused this sect of kidnapping, drugging, or brainwashing their children into staying in C.O.G. communes and perceiving their parents as creatures of the devil. It has been established that initiates are forced to sign a paper assigning all of their present and future incomes to the sect. Initially they must engage in long hours of Bible study, memorization, and group prayer; but they are taught almost exclusively the teaching of "Moses" David Berg. Berg has indicated approval of polygamy, incest, sexual activity for children, and has demanded complete obedience to C.O.G. leaders and hostility to the outside world. This is only one of the many hundreds of Jesus sects still thriving today; it is distinguished only by the sexual permissiveness condoned by its leader.

The more traditional Jesus sect keeps its male and female initiates apart; some to the degree that marriage or any sexual contact is not permitted. Asceticism is demanded, so that all one's energies are devoted to serving the Lord, or the leader of that particular cult. Drugs, including alcohol, cigarettes, and all chemical escapes are forbidden as well. Discipline is maintained through hours of study, memorization, meditation, enforced silence, isolation, and prayer.

Although they no longer receive much attention from the press, those in the Jesus movement continue to maintain much of their strength and enthusiasm. Many feel the Jesus people have grown up, and that more are becoming associated with established churches.

"Despite the efforts of Pat Boone, Roy Rogers, and Hal Lindsey, the amalgamation of the disaffiliated young with the churches has not been easy going. Many of the irreconcilable Jesus people have fled into the 'wilderness,' where they hope to survive in communal farms until the Second Coming. Many others have dropped unobtrusively back into suburban life, but shorn of illusions and hope."[3]

Following are some quotations of Sun Myung Moon: "I am your brain." "What I wish must be your wish." "My mission is to make new hearts, new persons." "The time will come . . . when my words will almost serve as law. If I ask a certain thing it will be done." "The whole world is in my hand, and I will conquer and subjugate the world." After hearing these statements, there is little wonder that many parents whose adolescents have "converted" accuse Moon of kidnapping, brainwashing, and slavery.

In the early seventies, Sun Myung Moon brought his message to America—and America obviously listened. His cult's income in this country alone for 1975 was estimated at $10 million. Reportedly this group has over thirty thousand members in the United States; ten thousand of them work full-time for Moon, recruiting, selling nuts and flowers on the streets or en-

---

[3]Richard J. Woods, "Jesus Freaks, Gurus and Dissent," p. 28. Copyright © 1974 by The Progressive, Inc. Reprinted by permission of *The Progressive*, Madison, Wis.

gaged in other fund raising activities. Most live in one of the over one hundred communes his followers have established.

A confidential advanced training manual of Moon's Unification Church states that Moon must become the richest and most powerful man in the world to achieve God's will. Moon is presently living on a huge estate in New York and driving an expensive limousine. He had to accept this automobile since, as his manual states, it came by itself "with a speed of two hundred miles per hour and said if Father didn't receive it, it would kill him."

When Moon appears, albeit infrequently, he speaks to his followers only in Korean, so many cannot understand his appeal. His delivery can best be described as emotional, complete with tears and karate chops; his dynamism springing from this and the fact that his followers perceive him as a divinity.

"Life in a Moonie commune offers a welcome refuge to those unwilling or unable to face the daily frustrations of life on the outside: no drugs, no drinks, no sex, no money, no problems, no choices, no decisions. From the team leader's cheerful 'Rise and shine!' in the sexually segregated dormitories to the last group songs and prayers at midnight, the Moonies rarely have to think for themselves. Full of religious fervor and newfound purpose, they follow orders and perform chores with gusto."[4]

Although the ads run in newspapers and the handouts and other literature on Moon's Unification Church sound relatively conventional, the esoteric teachings make it clear that Moon ("Messiah," "Master," "Father") must have dominion over America to subdue Communism, which he terms Satanism. Followers believe that America must come back to God, and God's words come through Moon.

Although they deny that their Messiah has political goals, converts do believe that our Constitution will be changed to conform to his theology—the Divine Principle. Moon published this text after alleged conversations with Jesus in a

---

[4]Berkeley Rice, "Honor Thy Father Moon," pp. 40–41, *Psychology Today*, Jan. 1976.

vision telling him that the second Messiah would be born in 1920 (his birthyear) in Korea (his birthplace). Moon teaches that since Satan seduced Eve, corruption began and that Jesus was to have started a pure race after marrying a perfect woman, but He was crucified. Now, he, the Second Messiah (but, he never quite identifies himself as such) is here to perfect the human race.

The Hare Krishna Society, composed of approximately five thousand members, requires of its missionaries much self-sacrifice and insulation from those not in the movement. Members believe that by selfless concentration and denial of material and sense gratifications they can be liberated from the karmic cycle. Many who enter the Krishna movement previously found life a painful search for something; they had "tried on" new causes, life patterns, and other religions and found them unsatisfactory. Krishna attracts confused adolescents because it lays down a predetermined plan for earthly happiness by guaranteeing spiritual freedom in the present and hereafter. This movement emphasizes the simple and austere, almost monastic life.

Young people are urged by some mystics to learn to control their destinies. They are instructed to study the ancient sciences in order to cope with our present times of anxiety and depression and the prevailing lack of credibility many associate with our political and spiritual leaders.

Attempting to deal with alienation and trying to understand the confusion and brutality prevalent in our society, adolescents continue to search for ways to alleviate stress and improve their lives. Many Eastern philosophies emphasize concentration, awareness, and peace of mind, and the focus is not materialistic or centered around a system of rewards and punishments—thus their appeal. Youngsters searching for eternal truths about our universe and their place in it often study Transcendental Meditation, Zen Buddhism, Yoga, Tai Chi Chuan, and other disciplines; many with a distinct oriental theme. Eastern philosophies are becoming more meaningful and accessible to us, and their cosmic and mystical aspects generate great interest. Several of these consciousness movements are centuries old and stress new depths of self-enlightenment, body awareness, and discovery of inner peace, fulfillment, and greater energy.

The "fad factor" is clearly involved. Certainly there are groupies who flit from TM to Zen to retreats with Yogis—following whatever is currently practiced by their peers. These people may be equated to those in the sixties who experimented with one mind-expanding drug after another. Those pursuing the human potential movement today appear more sensible, and as long as they do not lose their sense of perspective, the majority of these practices are not unhealthy and may even enhance reality.

Transcendental Meditation (a currently popular practice claiming worldwide practioners numbering between one and two million) when used properly is designed to alleviate anxiety and increase energy. Simply speaking, the practitioner is given a personal and secret "mantra" to repeat silently. This repetition is designed to control the mind's ideas which distract from concentration, thereby facilitating calmness and relaxation. Students are to meditate twenty minutes in the morning and late afternoon, usually before dinner. During meditation there is a marked decrease in the body's oxygen consumption, respiratory rate, and heart rate, and in patients with elevated blood pressure, there is often lower blood pressure. It also appears that the regular practice of meditation may lead to decreases in drug usage, alcohol consumption, and cigarette smoking. Young drug users are generally knowledgeable about the undesirable effects of drugs, and actually it is not difficult for most to discontinue use; the problem is motivating them to want to stop. Meditators usually learn as a group, and seem to exert influence on each other to discourage drug use, inferring that drugs interfere with the feelings and benefits of meditation.

Zen Buddhism, a prominent oriental cult, is probably more adaptable to American society than is Krishna. Exercises in Zen Buddhism are purported to help practitioners experience selflessness and may lead to a cessation of unhappiness and a state of peace and divine judgments. Zen is considered a way of liberation from convention rather than a religion or philosophy, and the emphasis is on naturalness which should thrive when one has lost artificiality and self-consciousness. In Zen each trainee must find his own way, since what someone else teaches is not the student's knowledge. The revelation that the world is elusive lies at the core of Buddhism; that which exists is impossible to grasp. Zen's qualities of directness, depth, humor, and beauty are alluring to the young, and the philosophy continues to extend toward becoming a strong power in the intellectual considerations of the Western world.

CASE HISTORY

Holly, age sixteen: "I guess I've always been interested in ways to control fate and destiny—and I've long been fascinated with those who claim psychic powers and occult knowledge. Another issue that has concerned me is immortality—and my Christian indoctrination hasn't provided answers I can accept. About a year ago a girl friend and I went to a fortune-teller and she astounded me with facts I thought no one knew but me. She further predicted that I was a bit of a psychic myself, and could use my gift for good or evil. I decided to investigate and one night found myself meeting with a coven of witches in a town not far from my own. They only let me observe, and when I saw them killing animals in their rites and doing some other unbelievable things, I became ill. I forced myself to stay until the end, and was asked by one who seemed to be the leader if I wanted to be initiated. The group gathered around me and shrieked 'Yes! Yes! Yes!' I was terrified. Apparently they had done some checking on me and knew of my interest. Well, I said I'd think about it; just because I was so scared and wanted to get away. They did and said some weird things, and all I want to do is to get back to normal and try to forget that freaky experience."

It is evident that witchcraft is prevalent and dynamic in America and its lore, ceremonies, and superstitions are fascinating to many young people. In the past few decades there has been a renewal of interest in all matters occult, particularly sorcery. Mysterious and clandestine teachings are often allowed to pass only between blood relatives or people who have been joined in sexual intercourse. Numerous "Satanistic" cults have been initiated in this country for the purpose of devil-worship. Their appeal is often directed to the young, particularly to the sexually frustrated and hostile who will participate in sadistic and gruesome acts for "kicks."

Witches, who generally reject Satanism and black magic, believe in realms beyond the physical and powers that are latent and inoperative in the majority of people. Their basic conflicts with orthodox religions are the beliefs in their own contact with the Beyond and their conception of the Deity as a hierarchy of gods and goddesses, governing various aspects of nature.

Life is changing rapidly, and witchcraft, with its consonance with nature and its creed: "Do what you will, so long as it hurts no one," is thought by many as more righteous and just than lists of "thou shalt nots."

Much of adolescents' search into unconventional religions and mysticism is to find something of meaning they felt their parents do not have in their lives: spiritual peace and joy.

12 Preventive Medicine in Doses Children Can Take

Since an adolescent's feelings of self-worth constitute the essence of his personality, his judgment of himself affects all aspects of his life, strongly influencing his use of his potentials. Parents, therefore, must encourage their youngster's belief in himself so he will succeed in becoming a contented, secure, and fulfilled individual.

Today's parents are ready for change since they have discovered that traditional childrearing practices and approaches to discipline have not produced secure and satisfying parent-child relationships. Parents need to learn to handle constructively the unavoidable conflicts that evolve as their youngsters mature.

In our Western culture the adolescent stage is particularly long because the preliminary measures required for autonomous adult status are greater than in less complex societies. The youngster thus usually faces an identity crisis —he may be dependent but expected to act independently; he regards himself and is regarded as neither child nor adult. In our society defining the adolescent's role is a dilemma to both parents and their youngsters.

Adolescents are generally exceedingly sensitive and most tend to live in extremes—happy one moment and miserable the next. The majority of young persons resist parental sympathy, help, and even understanding. They question their parents' dictates, oppose their restrictions, and defy their values. This may be because parents respond to their feelings in ways adolescents intensely despise—usually by disregarding, denying, reassuring, or brushing them aside. The knowledge that they may express their feelings to concerned and empathetic parents who may eventually help them create their own solutions will promote self-respect rather than resentment.

Parents should not make their adolescents' problems their own, although their concern and counsel may be sought. The problem can be classified as belonging to the child when he is prevented from satisfying a need and his behavior is a problem to him—not to his parents. For example, Tom is frustrated because he is having difficulty with his homework; Beth is unhappy because a boy she cared about broke a date with her; Rob is angry because he was not allowed to start as quarterback in a school football game. Parents should leave the responsibility for solving these problems with their children, in order for them to become more responsible and self-directing. Frequently well-intentioned parents feel that when their children are confused or upset they should offer solutions or reassurances. These responses usually abet the decline of their relationships with their adolescents who want to exercise their abilities to deal with their own concerns.

If parents try to understand the dynamics that account for a child's behavior when with his friends, they can look for certain signs signifying possible conflicts. A young person who continually fights and is unable to make and keep friends, one who finds fault with most of his peers—"Johnny is such a show-off," "Bob is a dummy"—along with the child who always feels he is being discriminated against or "picked on" illustrate cases of young people with low self-esteems. Children who withdraw from activities and want to be alone, often retiring to their rooms, may well be having difficulty making or sustaining friendships. If this situation persists, a parent should realize there is a probable difficulty and should try to discover causative factors behind the withdrawal.

During the decided shift at the preadolescent stage from acceptance of parental norms and standards to adoption of those of the peer group, it is natural for parents to be alarmed, particularly when this movement is accompanied by an increase in negativism directed toward the parents, as it frequently is. Parents may resent changes in their adolescents' attitudes and behaviors. Sometimes parents feel their positions are endangered and their authority threatened by their youngsters' emerging strength. Adolescents' drive for independence may disturb parents, who are aware of potential dangers their children may never suspect. The loosening of parental ties should be gradual and should accompany the development of maturity.

CASE HISTORY

Susan, age sixteen, thought that her weekend curfew of 11:00 p.m. was unfair. She tried many manipulatory techniques to get her parents to change it. She complained that all of her friends were allowed to stay out at least until midnight. Her parents reacted with empathy to her comments, but stated that they did not intend to change her curfew. They let her know that since she seldom came in on time they felt that she was not yet ready to assume the responsibility for regulating her own behavior. They told Susan that when she did not come home when she was supposed to it worried them, both because something could have happened to her and because she had not kept her word. They told her that when she had demonstrated to them that she could be more responsible, they would be willing to renegotiate.

When parents find their child involved with a truly undesirable group, they must intervene if at all possible. They should try to discover why their child began these associations, and while respecting his need for independence, provide appropriate guidance. Healthy friendships and peer group relationships make life more pleasant and growing up easier and help to prepare young people for various types of associations they will have later in life.

As people, we must consider how very lonely life would be without love. Unconditional love is usually cyclical—those who give love ultimately find it returned. Adults who do not love and accept themselves tend to distrust and reject their children. Parents need to critically examine their feelings about themselves since studies indicate a direct correlation between how accepting people are of themselves and their tolerance and acceptance of others. Those who seek opportunities to fulfill their potentials in areas other than family do not expect their child to gratify all of their needs. This leaves to the child the opportunity to explore and determine options available to him, instead of being used by his parents to satisfy their self-esteem.

Parents need to convey to their adolescents that they are trusted. This will prove the self-fulfilling prophecy—expect the goodness in your children, and this is what they will offer. The opposite also applies. If more parents were less judgmental, threatening, punitive, or even inappropriately reassuring, and if they listened to their children to help them clarify their feelings, they would be surprised by their youngsters' attitudinal changes.

CASE HISTORY

Peggy, age 14:	I don't really want to go to school tomorrow.
Mother:	I guess there are times you'd like to skip school.
Peggy:	I really hate school—it's too hard!
Mother:	The work is so difficult, sometimes you really hate going.
Peggy:	Oh, there are other reasons, too.
Mother:	Would you like to talk about them?
Peggy:	Not really; I guess it's the other kids.
Mother:	The other kids at school.

Peggy:	Yeah, I'm not that well liked, you know.
Mother:	It bothers you because you don't feel too popular with the other kids.
Peggy:	Yes, I really don't feel a part of any group, if you know what I mean.
Mother:	You'd sort of like to belong, but you don't know how to go about it.
Peggy:	Well, they work harder at school and do seem to take part in more of the activities than I do.
Mother:	You feel that's why they're more friendly with each other.
Peggy:	That could be it—maybe I should get in on some of the activities, and, as tough as it is, pull up the grades.
Mother:	That could be an answer.

Often parents become so involved in doing things *for* their child that they neglect seeing him as a person. Cooking meals, taking him to the orthodontist, sponsoring Scouts, saving for his education—these activities may assume so much consequence that he is neglected as a human being. Certainly parents can give their youngster wholehearted attention when needed to help alleviate some of his pressures and make him feel understood. If they communicate to their child that they have faith in his capacity for growth and maturity, his progress will be enhanced. Regressions are anticipated; each child's growth prototype will exhibit plateaus and declines and each will be unique. Youngsters must feel some degree of emotional safety to chance independence, exploration, and self-discovery. Probably unrealistic expectations and parental disapproval are most detrimental to an adolescent's secure psychological environment and feelings of competence.

Often an adolescent feels guilty about hostile feelings directed toward other family members. Assume that a child hit his younger brother for breaking a toy. The usual parental response is "You're not supposed to hit your little brother." Although this is a legitimate statement, he may also get the impression that he should not feel anger toward his brother. Since he must feel resentful in such an instance, he may become confused. He needs to know that he has permission to feel anger but not to hit. In other words, young people should learn from their parents that they may have feelings, but they must be responsible for their actions.

If a young person does not feel closely bound to his parents and that he is a significant member of his family, his main loyalty will be to his peers. This weakens parental influence. When an adolescent does not feel family involvement, it is likely that he is striving not to be dependent upon them. For this reason he will probably not feel responsible to them or in any way controlled by them. Usually it is the need for his parents' approval and for identification with the family that makes a youngster try to live up to their expectations. If expectations are judicious and attainable, parents' approval of his progress is a more significant part of discipline than is punishment for his failure.

Parents who impart and demonstrate honesty to their children provide a nurturing environment. This does not mean that trust will be established only if parents are open about all of their feelings; certainly some they will not wish to share and others would be detrimental to their children's psychological safety. Parents should convey that they are not disguising their feelings—children need to know that they can have confidence that what their parents say is true. Learning that intimate relations must be honest gives young people security to approach others spontaneously.

Children need to learn not to hide their unacceptable feelings by erecting "false fronts." If they are appreciated only for their consideration, compassion, and willingness to do for others, for example, they may learn to mask or repress negative inclinations. Superficially all will appear satisfactory, but this compliance often masks a lack of confidence and assuredness. Role playing assures that associations are somewhat counterfeit until the front is abandoned in favor of relating genuinely.

As a youngster approaches adulthood, it usually becomes increasingly important that he establish close relationships with people of both sexes, and certainly the young person without a strong sense of identity will have problems in forming alliances. A significant reason is that he feels insecure in the role or roles he is playing in his attempt to win acceptance by his peers.

Erikson pointed out, "the total sense of identity is an ideal which no one attains completely or achieves once and for always. Most people feel accepted and self-accepting in some aspects of their lives, and partially or totally rejected in others." Particularly toward the end of adolescence, earlier conflicts are intensified and the urgency of taking on a stable role is greatest. When identity is experienced, Erikson describes it as "a sense of being at home in one's body, a sense of 'knowing where one is going,' and an inner assuredness of anticipated recognition from those who count."[1]

Young people need to learn that a person and his behavior are distinct and independent. They should not be taught that if their behavior is bad, they are bad, and if it happens that their conduct is good, they are good people. If they learn no distinction and separation between acts and self, their personal worth can be revoked with any error of conduct. Since no young person consistently responds appropriately, he must formulate a sound appraisal of personal value so his feelings of esteem will not be so precarious and unstable. To preserve self-respect, parents should refrain from negative judgments which make children feel inadequate. Positive appraisals or labels also can be damaging because they do not help to separate a youngster from his acts. Instead of labeling, parents should relate their reactions to their children's behaviors: "I can't tolerate such a messy room." "I appreciate your mowing the lawn." "It makes me angry to see you hurt your little sister."

Young people who are encouraged to develop in-

---

[1]Erik Erikson, *Identity: Youth and Crisis,* p. 165.

dependence are frequently less conforming than those with rigid, restricting parents. We can infer from this that if parents keep their children dependent, they will later transfer this dependency to their peer group. Adolescents ideally have developed some internal control of their behavior. These controls usually develop as a result of the restrictions their parents set for them in their earlier years. Self-discipline helps young people form satisfying relationships with others.

Frequently an adolescent feels that he can best assert his independence by alienating and withdrawing from his parents. Instead he must learn to reach agreements with them on the behaviors that affect both him and other family members. Adolescents usually want as much freedom as is realistically possible, but they need to learn to deal with difficulties that lack of restrictions may bring into existence.

Methods of discipline, both rules for behavior and methods to enforce them, can vary radically so long as parents attempt to be fair and consistent and remember to treat their children with respect. They should try to remember to teach by example; too often parents tell their children to do one thing while they themselves are doing another. Limits must be set in order for families and society to survive. Most parents want their youngsters to comply with regulations because they are part of the children's value systems, rather than to accept them merely to avoid punishment. When children feel rules are just and reasonable, they are more likely to incorporate them in order to discipline themselves, and when family relations are cordial, members are generally more cooperative.

A family lifestyle that stresses equalitarianism, involving complementary roles of adults as well as youngsters in the family, usually results in increased harmony rather than conflict between generations. In the patriarchal system, still popular with many families, the father makes all important decisions and is the role model for his family, who (ideally) closely follows his direction. The problem with authoritarianism is that when the authority figure is absent, youngsters no longer feel obligated to follow his dictates. It further discourages self-reliance and may create rebellious behavior.

In our society of change, fathers and mothers often tend to enter the peer arena and try to relate to their children as friends rather than as parents. When young people no longer view their parents as authorities, values are likely to be integrated by experiences with peers rather than identification with parents. This is unfortunate since ideally parents should be responsible for teaching values and providing strong emotional guidance.

Overpermissiveness often makes a youngster feel unloved and anxious. A child can sense when his parents are uninvolved, and he frequently fails to learn self-discipline and mature decision making. Eventually those who provide their child with few or no limits reach a point where they can no longer tolerate his inconsideration and selfish behavior, and they may reject him when he most needs their support.

A democratic approach to discipline based on giving adolescents a voice in decisions directly affecting them usually creates more cooperative and self-reliant individuals. Research suggests that including young people in policy making helps them feel worthwhile, less resentful of limits, and more able to make responsible decisions.

Parents must guard against rearing "people pleasers": youngsters who have learned to meet others' expectations at the cost of their own integrities. They might instead teach their children to recognize their own powers to determine issues and encourage expression of their opinions and convictions. When young people realize their parents can tolerate their defeats and failures, they will be more willing to take chances and declare their personal beliefs. Parents who refrain from attempting to make their children feel guilt or shame for their values, statements, and actions will probably experience less resentment.

Adolescents often complain that their parents give them no privacy; they enter children's rooms without knocking, listen to telephone conversations, read letters, diaries, quiz friends, search dresser drawers—the list is endless. Nothing seems to make young people more resentful. Adults must learn to respect territorial rights. It is the lack of privacy that makes many young people want to leave home as early as possible and to be with their families infrequently during adolescent years. Parents who may be guilty of intruding probably have good intentions for their children's welfare and should begin to rectify the situation. No parents are without fault and they should look on their mistakes as opportunities for growth.

Epilogue

Unfortunately, we cannot "give" our children adequate security and self-esteem as easily as we provide them with new guitars, cars, or bicycles. But without these attributes we cannot expect them to listen to our teachings and ultimately set their own standards, disregarding those taught and practiced by their peers.

Since communication between the generations ranges in so many instances on a sliding scale from hostile to nonexistent, the adolescent may have no one but his peers to talk with. Particularly when his parents are prone to moralizing, judging, and preaching, an adolescent will take his troubles to his own group, whose advice may be followed simply because his peers are not judgmental.

Effective communication between parent and adolescent cannot begin on the child's sixteenth birthday, however. Parents frequently wonder why their children never come to them for counsel. But when this is not encouraged, developed, and nurtured from infancy into childhood and preadolescence, rarely does it miraculously appear at the onset of puberty.

Bibliography

Books

Brownmiller, Susan. *Against Our Will: Men, Women, and Rape.* New York: Simon and Schuster, 1975.

Bugliosi, Vincent, and Gentry, Curt. *Helter Skelter.* New York: W. W. Norton, 1974.

Constantine, Larry L., and Constantine, Joan M. *Group Marriage.* New York: Macmillan, 1973.

Cressey, Donald R., and Ward, David A. *Delinquency, Crime, and the Social Process.* New York: Harper and Row, 1969.

Deutsch, M. *The Disadvantaged Child.* New York: Basic Books, 1957.

Erikson, Erik. *Identity: Youth and Crisis.* New York: W. W. Norton, 1968.

Fleming, C. M. *Adolescence: Its Social Psychology.* New York: Grove Press, 1962.

Frank, Lawrence K., and Frank, Mary. *Your Adolescent at Home and in School.* New York: Signet, 1959.

Friedan, Betty. *The Feminine Mystique.* New York: Dell, 1963.

Ginott, Haim G. *Between Parent and Teenager.* Toronto: Macmillan, Collier-Macmillan Canada, 1969.

Glass, G. V., and Stanley, J. C. *Statistical Methods in Education and Psychology.* New York: Prentice-Hall, 1969.

Goldenson, Robert M. *The Encyclopedia of Human Behavior: Psychology, Psychiatry, and Mental Health.* New York: Doubleday & Co., Inc., 1970.

Gordon, Thomas. *Parent Effectiveness Training.* New York: Peter H. Wyden, 1970.

Havinghurst, Robert J., and Neugarten, Bernice L. *Society and Education,* 3d edition. Boston: Allyn and Bacon, 1967.

Hurwood, Bernhardt J. *Passport to the Supernatural.* New York: Taplinger, 1972.
Lair, Jess. *I Ain't Much, Baby—But I'm All I've Got.* New York: Doubleday, 1972.
Lingeman, Richard R. *Drugs from A to Z: A Dictionary.* New York: McGraw-Hill, 1969.
Louria, Donald B. *Overcoming Drugs: A Program for Action.* New York: McGraw-Hill, 1972.
Marin, Peter, and Cohen, Allan Y. *Understanding Drug Use: An Adult's Guide to Drugs and the Young.* New York: Harper & Row, 1971.
McAcree, C. P., et al., *Personality Factors in College Drug Users,* n.d.
McCary, James Leslie. *Human Sexuality.* Princeton: Van Nostrand, 1967.
O'Neill, Nena and O'Neill, George. *Open Marriage: A New Life Style for Couples.* New York: M. Evans & Co., Inc., 1972.
Olshaker, Bennett. *What Should We Tell the Kids?* New York: Dell, 1971.
Prather, Hugh. *I Touch the Earth; The Earth Touches Me.* New York: Doubleday & Co., Inc., 1972.
Reik, Theodor. *Curiosities of the Self.* New York: M. Wolff, 1965.
Roberts, Susan. *Witches U.S.A.* New York: Dell, 1971.
Rogers, Carl R. *On Becoming a Person.* Boston: Houghton Mifflin, 1961.
Sorensen, Robert C. *Adolescent Sexuality in Contemporary America.* New York: World, 1971.
Spock, Benjamin. *A Teenager's Guide to Life and Love.* New York: Pocket Books, 1971.
Watts, Alan W. *The Way of Zen.* New York: Vintage Books, 1957.
Wilderson, David, and Cox, Clair. *Parents on Trial.* New York: Pyramid Books, 1971.
Zolar. *The Encyclopedia of Ancient and Forbidden Knowledge.* Los Angeles: Nash, 1970.

Articles and Pamphlets

American School Health Association Committee on Drugs and Pharmaceutical Manufacturers Association. "Teaching about Drugs: A Curriculum Guide." 2d edition, 1972.
Beelick, Delbert B. "Sources of Student Satisfaction and Dissatisfaction." *Journal of Educational Research,* Sept. 1973.
Brickman, William W. "Drug Addiction and the Schools." *School and Society* Feb. 1971.

Brookover, W., et al. "Self-Concept of Ability and School Achievement." Bureau of Educational Research Services, Michigan State Univ., 1962.

"Children of Moses." *Newsweek,* Oct. 28, 1974.

Cornell, George W. "Those 'Guru' Cults—Religion or Exploitation?" *Reader's Digest,* Feb. 1976.

English, Clifford J. "Leaving Home: A Typology of Runaways." *Society,* July/Aug. 1973.

Finkelstein, Barbara J. "The Search for Identity—An Institutional Problem?" *Intellect,* Dec. 1973.

French, J. L. "Characteristics of High Ability Dropouts." *Bulletin of the National Association of Secondary School Principals,* 1969.

Gillingham, J. "A Study of Dropouts in Dade County, Florida, Public Schools." Dade County, Fla., Department of Research, 1974.

Gold, Robert E. "Early Steps Toward Preventing Drug Abuse." *PTA Magazine,* March 1970.

Graham, Augusta, "A Parent's Manifesto—Our Grievances," *PTA Magazine,* March 1970.

Gramick, Sister Jeannine. "The Myths of Homosexuality." *Intellect,* Nov. 1973.

Higgins, John W., and Katzman, Michael B. "Determinants in the Judgment of Obscenity." *American Journal of Psychiatry,* June 1969.

Hillman, Eugene. "Reconsidering Polygamy." *Commonweal,* Nov. 21, 1975.

Horn, Patricia, and the Editors of *Behavior Today.* "Street People —A Growing Urban Problem." *Psychology Today,* May 1975.

"Jesus '75: The Spirit Lives On." *Christianity Today,* Sept. 12, 1975.

Katz, Joseph. "Rearing Rads, Rebs, and Regulars." *PTA Magazine,* Aug. 1970.

Klaus, Hanna. "A Medical Cop-Out." *Sexual Behavior in America,* Aug. 16, 1975.

Lasseigne, Mary W. "A Study of Peer and Adult Influences on Moral Beliefs of Adolescents." *Adolescence* (1975), vol. 10, no. 38.

Marty, Martin E. "The Comet That Fizzled." *Christian Century,* Feb. 27, 1974.

McCracken, Samuel. "The Drugs of Habit and the Drugs of Belief." *Commentary,* Oct. 1971.

Novak, Michael. "Gay Is Not Liberation." *Commonweal,* May 23, 1974.

Otto, Herbert A. "Communes: The Alternative Life-Style." *Saturday Review,* April 24, 1971.

Powell, Robert, and Duggan, Dexter. "Liberation—In Whose Terms?" *Harper's Magazine,* May 1974.

Rice, Berkeley, "Honor Thy Father Moon." *Psychology Today.* Jan. 1976.

Rosenbaum, Veryl. "Guidelines for Parents Hoping to Survive Their Child's Adolescence." *PTA Magazine,* Nov. 1974.

Seligson, Marcia. "Can You Be More Sure of Yourself?" *Vogue,* June 1975.

Steffenhagen, Ronald A. "Drug Abuse and Related Phenomena: An Adlerian Approach." *Journal of Individual Psychology,* Nov. 1974.

Thomas, Charles W., Peterson, David N., and Zingraff, Matthew T. "Student Drug Use: A Re-Examination of the 'Hang Loose Ethic' Hypothesis." *Journal of Health and Social Behavior,* March 1975.

Thornburg, Hershel D. "An Investigation of a Dropout Program Among Arizona's Minority Youth." *Education,* Feb./March 1974.

Van Horn, Harriet. " 'Being in Love' Versus 'Having a Relationship.' " *Family Weekly,* November 2, 1975.

Vener, Arthur M., Stewart, Cyrus S., and Hager, David L. "Low Adolescent Use of Drugs." *School and Society,* Oct. 1971.

Woefel, Joseph. "Adolescent-Adult Bond." *School and Society,* Dec. 1971.

Woods, Richard J. "Jesus Freaks, Gurus and Dissent." *The Progressive,* June 1974.

Index